Strong Fathers, Strong Daughters Devotional

Meg Meeker, M.D.

Strong
Fathers,
Strong
Daughters
Devotional

52 Devotions
Every Father Needs

SALEM
BOOKS
an imprint of Regnery Publishing

Regnery Faith™ is a trademark of Salem Communications Holding Corporation; Regnery® is a registered trademark of Salem Communications Holding Corporation

Cataloging-in-Publication data on file with the Library of Congress
ISBN 978-1-62157-501-6

Some names have been changed to protect the privacy of individuals.

Published in the United States by
Salem Books
An imprint of Regnery Publishing
A Division of Salem Media Group
300 New Jersey Ave NW
Washington, DC 20001
www.SalemBooks.com

Manufactured in the United States of America

10 9 8 7 6 5 4 3 2

Books are available in quantity for promotional or premium use. For information on discounts and terms, please visit our website: www.Regnery.com.

To my beloved husband Walt,
my inspiration for writing about strong fathers.

CONTENTS

PART III
THE VIRTUES OF STRONG FATHERS

PART IV
THE HABITS OF STRONG FATHERS

PART V
THE IMPACT OF STRONG FATHERS

INTRODUCTION

I'd like to open this book with something that you might not expect—an apology.

As men, many of you have been led to believe that aside from bringing home a paycheck and maybe knocking in a nail here or there, you're not much needed at home.

You might even doubt yourself—you don't really know how to be a dad.

You might think your wife doesn't listen to you, your kids don't listen to you, so you might as well just shut up.

You might feel that you bunk at your home. You don't actually *live* there.

So let me say right now: I'm sorry.

I'm sorry because I was there when the modern Feminist movement, and the pop culture that has adopted it, derided and degraded masculinity.

I'm here to help you regain what is rightfully yours—your role as an involved father.

I know you are a good man because you picked up this book, because you want to be closer to your kids. You're on the right track.

Let this truth sink deep into your being: *you have what it takes to be a great dad to your kids.*

How do I know? Because I've talked to dads of every description: NFL football players, Joe Lunchbuckets, and high-flying executives.

I've seen you with a temper that's out of control, a depression that has swallowed you up, an affair that has split your family apart, and drinking habits that have landed you in jail.

I've seen you turn away from each and every one of these temptations, and draw on a God-given fatherly strength and tenacity.

Everything you need to be a great dad to your daughter is hard-wired into your soul. It's part of being a man. You just need to find it.

Believing you have failed is easy. It's easy to give up and go away.

But as you know, real men don't quit.

Yes, it takes work. A good marriage is harder than having an affair (for a while at least). But a good marriage is what you were made for—and it's better than any affair can be.

Being a good parent takes work. But fatherhood is the greatest adventure a man can ever have.

I hope in this book to help you along in that adventure—to help you discover what's within you; how to be the great dad your daughter needs you to be.

I say this as a doctor who has spent decades listening to girls talk about their fathers—and I say it as a Christian who believes that your faith is profoundly important to helping you be the best man and father you can be.

Bible scholars tell us that after the Old Testament was given to God's people, God went silent—silent!—for three hundred years. Before these centuries of silence, God told His people something incredibly profound: "See, I will send you the prophet Elijah before that great and dreadful day of the Lord comes. He will turn the hearts of the fathers to their children and the hearts of the children to their fathers; or else I will come and strike the land with a curse."

His last words, before the coming of His own Son, were to you fathers. Who you are, what you believe, what you say and do with your children matters. It *really* matters.

PART I

THE NEED FOR STRONG FATHERS

Week 1: Calling Strong Fathers

Week 2: Today Is a New Day

Week 3: You Have What It Takes

Week 4: You Are Not Alone

CALLING STRONG FATHERS

The glory of children is their fathers.
—Proverbs 17:6, ESV

I don't know why you picked up this book. Maybe someone recommended it; or perhaps your wife or a friend gave it to you. I don't know if you're examining it in a bookstore or skimming it while riding on a commuter train.

But if you are reading these words, three things are almost certainly true:

1. You have a daughter you love.
2. You are a conscientious man with a good heart.
3. You desperately want to connect with your daughter and help her become a healthy adult.

It could be that your daughter is a teen or young adult who's struggling. You've tried everything you can think of to help her. To date, nothing has worked. Maybe you're at your wits' end.

It could be that your daughter is still a young and reasonably compliant child—but she's growing faster than bamboo in a tropical rain forest. And while you can't shield her forever from every pain of life as she rockets toward adulthood, you want to spare her unnecessary heartache.

I don't have to tell you our world is cruel to girls. Every day our daughters are exposed to ugly realities. The media assaults their worth. Peers and predators make them targets of verbal, emotional, and sexual abuse.

Often by the time a troubled, hurting girl shows up in my office, she's depressed, addicted, infected (with an STD), or pregnant. Some of my patients have run away from home. Others are just waiting for the opportunity.

What's the solution to this "daughter crisis"? It depends on whom you ask. Politicians call for more studies and new laws. Mental health professionals call for more counseling and empowerment programs. Women's groups call for more sex education, birth control, and federal funding.

I'm calling for *stronger fathers*.

This is also the call of your daughter: "Be strong for me, Dad. Protect me. Teach me. Show me the way." Girls think such things constantly, even when they can't or won't say them overtly. As wise King Solomon observed (in the verse cited above), the glory of a daughter is her father. In my book *Strong Fathers, Strong Daughters: 10 Secrets Every Father Should Know*, I expressed it this way: "If you could see yourself as [your daughter] sees you, even for ten minutes, your life would never be the same" (pp. 4–5).

From experience, I know that when fathers don't engage, when they fail to offer the masculine strength and guidance a mother is unable to provide, something goes wrong within the soul of a girl. I know this from thirty-plus years of practicing pediatric and adolescent medicine. I know this also from a mountain of scientific data. This is not an opinion; it's a fact: girls *get* better and *do* better and *are* better when they are guarded and guided by strong, involved fathers. Conversely, girls don't do well—they get lost and in trouble—when their dads go AWOL or become distracted.

No wonder the apostle Paul wrote this sobering warning in the New Testament: "Fathers, do not exasperate your children, so that they will not lose heart" (Colossians 3:21, NASB).

Heed the sacred warning: "Do not exasperate your children." How does a father exasperate or discourage his daughter and cause her to lose heart?

I've seen this loss of heart happen in two primary ways: (1) when a dad is guilty of being harsh and making unreasonable demands; and (2) when a dad is guilty of gross inattention and neglect.

But I've also seen something else. I've seen fathers who nurture their daughters and enjoy great relationships with them. They do this by heeding the divine call to move strongly into their daughters' lives. These girls are heartened, encouraged, and brimming with confidence.

The place to begin is with this essential truth: God is calling *you*. Being a father is a divine summons. This call transcends what I think as a doctor. It's bigger even than what your daughter wants or needs.

Sadly, many men have difficulty hearing and embracing this high and noble calling. That's because for decades fathers have been mocked and demeaned. Cultural voices ridicule your authority and deny your importance. Internal voices challenge your competence and suggest your efforts will be futile.

I want to encourage you to turn away from all that noise and listen to that other Voice.

Being a strong father is a high and holy calling, but it's not a walk in the park. Being a dad is always tough, sometimes even terrifying. But like any great and worthy cause, when the risks are great, the rewards are even greater.

Late in life, Abraham was called by God to leave his homeland, go to a faraway place, and trust that his infertile, elderly wife would give him a son. He risked looking like a fool. But because he faithfully followed God's call, the nation of Israel was born.

Moses was called by the Almighty to lead his fellow Israelites out of Egypt. He risked death, rejection, and failure. But because he went, millions found freedom and made their way to the Promised Land.

Paul was called to preach the Good News to people across Asia and Europe. He risked his reputation and his life, enduring great hatred and abuse for announcing a message of love. But because he heeded the call of God, countless people through the ages have found hope and redemption.

Instead of choosing to make excuses, these men chose to make a difference. This is the mark of a great man.

Being "all in" when it comes to being a father to your daughter is as important as anything you'll ever do.

Will you heed the call?

PRAY

God, there's so much I don't understand about being a father—especially being the father of a daughter. But I have to believe You entrusted me with this precious child for a reason. And the truth is, if I don't step up to the plate, who will? If I don't answer the call to guard her and guide her through life, who will? I don't want to exasperate my daughter and cause her to lose heart. So please give me wisdom. And please supply courage. I want to be the kind of father who makes his daughter proud and who points her in the right way. Amen.

FLEX YOUR DAD MUSCLES

Take a few minutes and write out a list of your *hopes and dreams* for your daughter, such as:

- I want my daughter to know at the core of her being that she is loved unconditionally by God and by me.
- I want my daughter to value honesty and to grow into a woman of integrity.
- I want to help my daughter become discerning when it comes to evaluating cultural ideas, invitations from peers, and potential friends and boyfriends.

Then make a separate list of the *challenges* your daughter is currently facing. For example:

- My daughter is painfully shy and lacks self-confidence.
- My daughter is struggling in school.
- My daughter is beautiful and people only seem to notice and comment on her appearance.

Take your lists, review them, pray about them, and then set them as an action plan for your role as a father.

Week 2

Today Is a New Day

Is anything too hard for the Lord?
—Genesis 18:14, NIV

I want to say a word to the fathers who feel like they've blown it.

Let's say, generally speaking, you have a good relationship with your daughter. But last night at bedtime, you had a bad moment. You flew off the handle and made her sob uncontrollably. Now you feel like a jerk, and she's avoiding you.

Or perhaps it's a bigger issue. You didn't just have a bad moment. You've had a bad year—or two. Perhaps your daughter is in trouble or your relationship with her isn't exactly "warm." And maybe the deeper, uglier truth is that you know you are largely culpable for the status quo.

You didn't mean for any of this to happen, of course. But without even trying, you became too *something*—too busy, too obsessed with work, too distracted at home, too harsh, too controlling, too laissez-faire, too selfish, too careless with your words.

Maybe you did one (or even several) of those things for much too long, so that now you've got a royal mess on your hands. You're filled with hopelessness and facing a new batch of *toos*—*It's too late. I've failed her too many times. I'm too stuck in my ways to change. The situation has gotten too toxic.*

Here's what I wrote in *Strong Fathers, Strong Daughters*: "Even if you feel that it's too late, that she's too far gone from you, run to find her. It doesn't matter how old you are or how old she is. She is still your daughter. You are still her father" (p. 233).

I can't pretend to know what kind of situation you're in. And I surely can't guarantee a wonderful outcome for you, much less promise a repaired relationship by a certain date. But I will share four things that have helped me, as well as many of the fathers I know, when things seem especially bleak.

Look back. There is value in reviewing where we've been. Happy memories can fill our hearts with joy. For this reason you should rehearse and retell all your fun family stories again and again. They're helpful when hard times come. They serve to remind us, "Life wasn't always like this."

In a similar way, hard memories, while not fun to ponder, can also be useful. If we're wise, negative incidents in our past can serve as warnings. That's why so many of the Hebrew psalms recount Israel's worst failures. Our painful experiences contain valuable lessons, if we'll only search for them.

It's important to look back and laugh. We should also look back and be sobered. But the one thing we must resist doing when looking back is wallowing in regret. Beating yourself up over things that are unchangeable serves no good purpose. What's done is done. You can't unsay words or undo actions. So what *can* you do?

Look within. When you find yourself in an introspective mood and perhaps moving toward a place of unhealthy regret, stop and examine your heart. Ask yourself, *Have I sincerely sought forgiveness—from God and from my daughter (or anyone else I've hurt)? Have I taken responsibility for the things I shouldn't have done, and also for the things I ought to have* *done but didn't?* If you've answered yes to those questions, that's all you can do. You can't erase or rewrite the past, but you can begin writing a new future right now. If today is not exactly a "do-over," at least it's a new day, another chance.

Look forward. If you remember the story of the apostle Paul, you'll recall he was a man with quite a past. As a young adult, he was devout in his Judaism to the point of being fanatical. He participated in arresting Christians and endorsed the execution of their leaders.

Yet when Paul himself was unexpectedly, miraculously converted, he experienced a breathtaking transformation. This great enemy of the Christian faith became its most ardent defender. Though at times Paul must have been haunted by certain details of his past, his mind-set was clear: "I focus on this one thing: Forgetting the past and looking forward to what lies ahead" (Philippians 3:13, NLT).

This is a great principle for fathers who feel like they've made too many mistakes. Instead of focusing on all the wrong things you did or all the positive things you failed to do, look forward. Glean whatever lessons you can from your failures and move on. Focus on what you can do as you move into the future. Ask yourself, *What one thing can I do today?*

Look up. In my book, the eighth "secret" of being a strong father is to teach your daughter Who God is. In that chapter I point out that every dad forgets recitals or loses his temper because no dad is perfect. Every father needs to have a "bigger, better father" at his side.

God is that Father. He's the One we can turn to when we blow it. The promise of the Bible is that when we humbly acknowledge our mistakes and shortcomings to God, He is faithful to forgive us (1 John 1:9) and give us another chance.

God is also the Father we can turn to when things seem the most hopeless. Look again at the verse at the beginning of this chapter: "Is anything too hard for the Lord?" (Genesis 18:14, NIV). It's a divine, rhetorical question that God asks of the skeptical heart. Or as Christ said in Mark 10:27, "All things are possible with God" (NIV).

You might have blown it in a moment of weakness. Or you might be coming out of a long season of neglectfulness.

But because of the power and goodness of God, there's hope. It's not too late. The situation is not too far gone. Today is a brand new day.

PRAY

God, I can think of a thousand moments—maybe ten thousand—when I said or did the wrong thing. I rest in the promise of Your forgiveness and thank You for Your grace and mercy. Help me this day. Give me the humility to see where I need to make amends. Give me the courage to start anew with my daughter. Give me the hope and trust that You are at work in ways I can't see. Amen.

FLEX YOUR DAD MUSCLES

If you've had failures as a father, remember that today is a new day and you can take steps to make things right. First, pray for humility. If your relationship with your daughter is badly damaged, you might want to get advice from your wife or pastor. But if possible, go to your daughter—*run* to her. (Use the phone only if she's far away, but avoid texting or e-mailing.) Sit with her. If she's small, put her in your lap and hold her. If she's older, sit face to face. Take full responsibility for any wrong words, actions, attitudes, or tones of voice. Name your failures. Tell her you're sorry. Look her in the eyes. Ask her to please forgive you.

Be careful about making promises like "I will never do such a thing again." That's a noble intention but a dangerous statement to make. Future failures after such promises do incalculable damage to a daughter's heart. Instead, tell her you want desperately to change and will work hard to do so. Tell her you want more than anything to regain her trust and respect. Assure her of your love.

There is no stronger lesson in humility than a dad who is willing to admit the error of his ways. When you do this, you teach her not to play the victim, point the finger, or to justify or rationalize her own wrong actions.

You Have What It Takes

For I can do everything through Christ,
who gives me strength.
—Philippians 4:13, NLT

The number one question of men is not *Is the game on?* or *What's for dinner tonight?* or *Are we out of beer?* According to bestselling author John Eldredge, it's *Do I have what it takes?*

A man wrestles with this question all the time. He asks, *Can I pull off this deal? Land that job? Win her attention and affection? Start my own business? Support a growing family? Complete a triathlon?*

Men routinely ask some version of this question when dealing with their daughters: *Can I be the kind of father she needs? Can I figure out how to get her through this dark time? Will I be able to protect her? How can I survive this silly phase, this boy-crazy season of her life, this "I hate myself, you, and everything else" stage, this diva phase?*

Here's what I want to say to you: when it comes to fatherhood, the answer is yes. You have what it takes for three very simple reasons:

1. *You are a creature made in the image of God* (Genesis 1:26), you have a heart that is able to love. You have a mind that is

able to think. You have a will that is able to act. In your essential humanity, you have all that. You clearly have what it takes. But there's more.

2. *You are a man.* I know it is politically incorrect to say this, but my medical career and my experience as a wife and mother have confirmed this truth: every bit of your manliness—your strength, your masculine perspective, and your fatherly guidance—will be needed to raise a healthy daughter.

3. *You have maturity.* Even if you fear you're not mature enough for the sobering responsibilities of fatherhood, guess what? You are more mature than your young daughter.

I can hear the protest, "Yes, Dr. Meg, but being a father is a scary business. I've never done this. I'm not wise enough!"

Let me remove some of the pressure. Your daughter doesn't need King Solomon. She doesn't need you to be rich or to be a genius or to be anything that you aren't. God decided she needs *you.*

Are there things you don't know? Of course! And that will always be true. So keep learning, but just as important, pass on the things you *do* know. You have a lifetime's worth of experience.

At the end of his first letter to the church at Corinth, the apostle Paul gave this stirring command: "Be watchful, stand firm in the faith, act like men, be strong. Let all that you do be done in love" (1 Corinthians 16:13–14, ESV).

"Act like men, be strong." Here's the question: Do you really believe God would have given such a command—and do you think He would have given you your daughter—if He didn't believe you have what it takes?

You don't have to be a millionaire or a genius to be a strong father, but you have to be *available*, you have to be willing to *engage*. A successful dad is a dad who takes an active role in his daughter's life.

In *Strong Fathers, Strong Daughters*, I wrote:

You might not be able to single-handedly change popular culture or reform school curricula, but what you say and do, the
example you set, and the leadership you provide can absolutely
keep your daughter on the right track—or put her back on it.
Your influence is that important. (p. 233)

In other words, you have what it takes.

PRAY

God, I pray that through Your grace, I might have greater faith
in You and greater confidence in the abilities You have given me.
With Christ's help, I know I can do what I need to do, especially
when it comes to being a father to my daughter. Amen.

FLEX YOUR DAD MUSCLES

Take stock of your strengths, abilities, blessings, and experiences—things that you can call on in raising your daughter; make
a list and reflect on it. Your list might look something like this:

STRENGTHS

My great love for my daughter

My great love for her mother

My experience as an athlete (persistence, grit, determination)

My skill as a hunter (patience, a willingness to be silent and watch, my knowledge of nature)

The example of my own father

My faith

An inquisitive, practical, problem-solving mind

A compassionate heart

A desire to protect those I love

Week 4

You Are Not Alone

And be sure of this: I am with you always,
even to the end of the age.
—Jesus Christ, in Matthew 28:20, NLT

E verybody talks about how difficult being a parent is. But few people talk about how lonely it can be.

I know from countless interactions with parents that mothers and fathers of special needs kids feel this loneliness acutely, as do single parents. And all parents feel it to a degree when their children are struggling.

The internal voices during such times can be stern and cold: *Nobody wants to hear your sob story. Suck it up. Deal with it on your own.*

And the voices can be brutal: *How could you let this happen? Clearly, you're not going to win Father of the Year award. Come to think of it, why don't you go ahead and turn in your Dad Card? Nobody else's daughter has this problem.*

Perhaps you hear such voices—or others like them.

If so: tune them out. They're not true. You're not the only father who's struggling, not by a long shot. And don't buy the lie that someone else—a neighbor, church member, or coworker—is the perfect father. That's not the case. As I often remind the parents of my patients, even God Almighty, the one perfect Father, has messed-up kids.

There's no such thing as a perfect father. And your daughter doesn't want one.

And remember this: you don't have to make this journey alone.

Every dad, at some point, will need encouragement and reinforcements.

Even the strongest athletes get tired, and dads, like ballplayers, need a team around them to succeed—that team can include your wife, teachers, pastors, your own parents, a whole variety of people. I love what Woodrow Wilson once said: "I not only use all the brains that I have, but all I can borrow."

The truth is, you're *not* alone. Besides all the people around you, there is the astounding declaration of the Judeo-Christian Scriptures that God is omnipresent.

In the New Testament, Christ is introduced as *Immanuel*, a name that means "God with us." At the end of His earthly ministry, He gave this assurance: "I am with you always" (Matthew 28:20, NLT). And not long before that, He promised the faithful He would send His Spirit to live in their hearts. Christ called the coming Spirit the "Helper," insisting He will "be with [His followers] forever" (John 14:16, ESV).

If all these mind-boggling claims and statements are true (and, for the record, I am convinced they are), then you are *not* alone. God is with you 24/7, whatever your struggle or need. Help is available. The Almighty, the Helper, is only a prayer away.

What about the rest of your team members?

Your wife. Years ago, Father Theodore Hesburgh of Notre Dame famously said, "The most important thing a father can do for his children is to love their mother." His point was that a strong marriage is a father's best tool for raising strong, healthy kids. It's exactly what the Hebrew Scriptures say: "Two people are better off than one, for they can help each other succeed. If one person falls, the other can reach out and help. But someone who falls alone is in real trouble" (Ecclesiastes 4:9–10, NLT). Being on the same page with your wife is a huge advantage.

Even if you are divorced, your daughter will benefit if you work with her mother as an ally rather than an adversary. I know, given circumstances, this might be easier said than done, but I've seen, among the parents of my patients, how sensitivity, respect, and constructive compromises can go a long way.

Other fathers. Get to know the dads of your daughter's friends; you'll inevitably swap stories and learn something as a result. I've seen men become better, more attentive fathers by bouncing ideas off each other. As it says in Proverbs 27:17: "Iron sharpens iron, and one man sharpens another" (ESV).

A support group. Many churches have support groups for young mothers, single fathers, parents of special needs children, and so on. Many parents find friendship, instruction, and renewed hope by coming together to celebrate and commiserate, to share tips and say, "You too? You mean I'm *not* the only one with this problem?" Joys shared, as the old saying goes, are joys multiplied. Sorrows shared are sorrows minimized.

Counselors and medical professionals. In crisis situations, there are doctors and therapists with the special training who can help you. Listen to your gut. If you are sensing, "This is too big, I/we need professional help," follow your instincts.

Here's the bottom line: you are *not* alone. God not only made you a father, He gave you a family, a church, a community that is there for you to use, and He means you to use it.

PRAY

God, thank You for making me a father and for the help You provide as I find my way. I pray that I might always remember that You are with me, that I can always turn to You, and that You have provided me with people I can rely on. Give me the humility to admit when I'm struggling, and help me to seek support when I need it. Amen.

FLEX YOUR DAD MUSCLES

Here are three quick projects to reinforce the fact that you are not alone:

1. Memorize Christ's promise: *"And be sure of this: I am with you always, even to the end of the age."* Remembering this eternal truth will produce peace in your soul.
2. Get to know the dads of your daughter's closest friends. Not only might their friendship enhance your life, your shared experiences of fatherhood might provide comfort and useful advice.

3. Talk to your own dad, or reflect on your experiences with him, and think of how you can use his fatherly wisdom—or his fatherly mistakes—in your relationship with your daughter.

PART II

THE PRIORITIES OF STRONG FATHERS

Week 5: The Priority of Family

Week 6: The Priority of Faith

Week 7: The Priority of Love

Week 8: The Priority of Integrity

Week 9: The Priority of Example

Week 10: The Priority of Forethought

Week 11: The Priority of Peace

Week 5

THE PRIORITY OF FAMILY

*Those who bring trouble on their families
will have nothing at the end.*
—Proverbs 11:29, GNT

One of the most devastating things a father can do is put work or hobbies or trivial pursuits above his family.

You might remember the 1991 Steven Spielberg film *Hook*. It stars the late Robin Williams as Peter Banning (Peter Pan, the boy who vowed to *never* grow up). But Peter has grown up. What's more, he's become a driven, workaholic businessman. Right at the outset of a family vacation to London, Peter's latest deal, a $5 billion corporate takeover, begins to unravel.

As Peter works feverishly to rescue his deal, his wife Moira grabs his cell phone and hurls it out the window into the snow. He's shocked and angry, until he hears her say these sobering words:

> Peter...your children love you. They want to play with you. How long do you think that lasts? Soon Jack may not even want you to come to his games! We have a few special years with our children, when they're the ones that want us around. After that

you're going to be running after them for a bit of attention. It's so fast, Peter. It's a few years and it's over. And you are not being careful. And you are missing it!

What a chilling thought—to miss the brief window of time when your daughter is most in need of your love and attention. I don't want that for anyone, and you don't want that for yourself. So let's think together for a few moments about *the priority of family.*

Our priorities are whatever things or activities or relationships we value most. So how can a man tell what he values?

Here are some diagnostic questions for evaluating your priorities:

- What gets and keeps my *attention*? Where does my mind go when I'm not engaged in a mandatory activity? The fact is, we all think and daydream about the things we care about most.
- What dominates my *conversation*? Remember, talk is cheap, and it's easy to *say* certain things are important. Anyone can "talk a good game" in the short-term. Over time, though, what topics do I return to again and again? What do I talk about most? What sorts of things do I continually tweet or post online?
- What fills me with *passion*? When and where do I get animated and excited? What lights me up or makes me come alive or perhaps even moves me to the point of tears?
- What are the things I gladly spend my *money* on—maybe without even thinking twice? Possessions are necessary. Hobbies are fun. We all need some outlet for recreation. But what does it say about my priorities if I am willing to pour money into a hunting camp or a "man cave" but am reluctant or unwilling to set aside funds for experiences with my daughter or my family?

- Where does my time *go*? This is maybe the clearest indicator of all. It's a blunt but true reality: we make time to do the things that matter most to us.

Are you squirming yet? That's a tough list—not for those who are fainthearted. But truth be told, most people squirm when faced with these questions.

The point here is not to beat yourself up. The goal is simply to assess. As Sigmund Freud noted, "Being entirely honest with oneself is a good exercise." (It's not always fun, but it's good.)

Since you're reading this book, you probably *want* your daughter and your family to be your top priority. If an honest assessment shows they're not, the good news is you can start again today.

Page 28 of *Strong Fathers, Strong Daughters* provides an explanation of why time with your daughter is so important: "From the moment you set eyes on her wet-from-the-womb body until she leaves your home, the clock starts ticking. It's the clock that times your hours with her, your opportunities to influence her, to shape her character, and to help her find herself—and to enjoy living."

Time is what your daughter wants most from you. Nothing communicates the priority of family more than the willingness to spend relaxed time with her. Nothing makes a girl feel more valuable than recognizing her father enjoys her company. Knowing that you want her to join you in your everyday activities—when you do chores, run errands, stop at your office for a moment, or just take a walk—lets her know that you really enjoy being with her. This will make a huge impact on her sense of value.

You don't have to continue to be a busy, driven, scattered, preoccupied dad who is there but not *really* there. You don't have to look back one day and say, "If only…" or wistfully ask with Dr. Seuss, "How did it get so late so soon?"

Make your family a top priority. Don't put it off. "You may delay," Benjamin Franklin once warned, "but time will not."

PRAY

Lord, I need help. My priorities need work. Without meaning to, I've put trivial things ahead of the truly important things. I'm sorry about that. I pray that with the help of Your grace that I might properly reorder my priorities, putting my family before all else but You. Amen.

FLEX YOUR DAD MUSCLES

Make a special date with your daughter. Ask her what she'd like to do (within reason, of course). Then set aside a night or a Saturday and simply *be* with her. Don't spend those hours checking scores on your cell phone or making work phone calls. Don't zone out. Be there. Be attentive. Be fully engaged. Be all in.

If she is little and wants to have a dress-up tea party, do it. If she wants to go eat bad pizza and play games with a lot of other screaming kids, do it. If she's older and wants to go eat overpriced sushi, do it. If she wants to drive three hours to see a big concert featuring her favorite boy band, do what you have to do to make that happen.

Ask her questions. Talk to her. Listen to her. Be silly. Listen to her favorite songs on the radio and sing together. Tell her stories from your past. Have fun.

Nothing communicates "You matter, you are important, you are my precious priority" more than a cheerful willingness to spend time with your daughter.

Week 6

THE PRIORITY OF FAITH

*Fathers, do not exasperate your children; instead, bring them
up in the training and instruction of the Lord.*
—Ephesians 6:4, NIV

In *Strong Fathers, Strong Daughters*, I make the bold statement that "God is good for girls."

Our culture increasingly rolls its collective eyes at claims like that. Many media elites label religion—especially denominational Christianity—as regressive, unintelligent, even psychologically harmful. Lest I be accused of bias, let me say I agree that some people of faith, through messed-up motives and misguided actions, have given credence to such charges.

But let me also note that I've seen the power of authentic faith. I've read scientific studies and interacted with thousands of girls and young women as patients or as friends. I can cite a mountain of research and a pretty big hill of real-life examples from my personal experience to make the case that your daughter needs *you* to help her grow in faith and come to a clearer understanding of God.

If that's not enough, fathers have a clear biblical mandate to bring up their kids "in the training and instruction of the Lord."

But for some dads this raises a conundrum: *If my own faith is shaky or nonexistent, how can I help my daughter spiritually?* As the late Howard Hendricks correctly observed: "We cannot impart what we do not possess." Christ put the issue in question form: "Can one blind person lead another? Won't they both fall into a ditch?" (Luke 6:39, NLT). No man wants to be that father who hypocritically says to his daughter, "Do as I say, not as I do."

If faith is good for daughters, then wouldn't it be true that faith is also good for dads? Is it possible that faith needs to be a bedrock value of every father? I want to challenge you to wrestle with this topic and ask yourself, "What are my spiritual views and values? What do I believe about God?"

You may not be sure how to answer these questions. That's okay. The fact that you're reading this devotional tells me you're open to the question of faith. Don't give up the search. In fact, seek to cultivate the following habits:

Read the Bible. The Bible itself says, "Faith comes from hearing, and hearing through the word of Christ" (Romans 10:17, ESV). Our faith in God grows the more we pay attention to what He has revealed about Himself in the pages of Scripture and through Christ.

Sadly, many people reject the Bible without even reading it. They dismiss it solely on the basis of what others have said. I would counter by saying, "Don't take the word of others. Read it for yourself."

The Old and New Testaments are not a haphazard collection of disparate writings. They comprise one continuous story. The first book of the Bible tells of God's creation of the world and humanity's rebellion against Him. The next sixty-four books of the Bible unveil God's redemptive plan in history, culminating in the coming of Christ. The last book of the Bible gives us a glimpse of the future restoration of all things. It's one epic story, and it needs to be read that way with a thoughtful, humble, inquisitive mind (and preferably a prayerful one).

Pray. There are frequent encouragements to prayer in the Bible. For instance: "Devote yourselves to prayer with an alert mind and a thankful heart" (Colossians 4:2, NLT). But many men feel they don't know how to pray—they feel self-conscious, intimidated, ignorant. But prayer is simply conversing with God—and it's a conversation He wants to have. James 4:8 says, "Come close to God, and God will come close to you" (NLT).

What should you say to the Almighty in prayer? Whatever's on your heart. If God seems far away and talking to Him feels like talking to an imaginary friend, ask Him to reveal Himself to you. When you make poor choices, humbly confess your failures. When you are grateful, express this to God. When you have needs or concerns, ask for help. When you don't know what to do, ask for guidance. And, as in any good conversation, we shouldn't do all the talking. It is not only good, it is necessary in prayer to sit still and listen for God's voice.

Read spiritual classics. If you are one of those who are skeptical when it comes to the subject of faith, C. S. Lewis's *Mere Christianity* may help you as it has helped millions. More recent books like Tim Keller's *The Reason for God* or Lee Strobel's *The Case for Faith* are also excellent. (By the way, both Lewis and Strobel were confirmed atheists who each came to faith after an honest, rigorous, intellectual search.)

If you have a negative view of spirituality or a bad taste for religion, ask yourself why. Has this always been the case? Is your doubt or disillusionment due to a negative experience with church or with people of faith? Was your faith in God shattered by a devastating life event? If so, perhaps Philip Yancey's *Disappointment with God* would be helpful to you.

Practice your faith. "If you believe God exists, don't stop there. Ask yourself: What difference does it make if I do believe in God?" (*Strong Fathers, Strong Daughters*, p. 195). Let your faith propel you to serve others. Reflect your faith in your behavior—if you tend to be impatient, ask God for more patience; if you have a tendency to fly off the handle, trust God to make you gentler. One of Israel's great prophets said it best: "He has told you, O man, what is good; and what does the LORD require of you but to do justice, and to love kindness, and to walk humbly with your God?" (Micah 6:8, ESV).

God is good for girls. The research, which I cite in my other books, shows unmistakably that religious faith is an enormous benefit to children and teens (and yes, adults).

Your daughter needs to see that God is the ultimate Dad, the One she can turn to and trust in when you're not around.

As a father, God is your copilot. He can help you guide a safe course for yourself and your family.

PRAY

God, help me with my faith as I strive to learn more about You, draw near You, and have confidence in You. Help me to be a faithful father so I can pass a strong faith on to my daughter. Amen.

FLEX YOUR DAD MUSCLES

Faith is a very personal thing, but if you look at most of the great religions of the world, it's not really "private." Faith in God always involves a community of people struggling *together* to know and serve Him: to mourn together, to celebrate together, to encourage, instruct, remind, and challenge one another. It's no accident that Christ created a *church*. He was not a philosopher passing on advice to individuals but rather the Son of God with a mission to create and expand a community of believers.

Make the commitment to attend a church or temple this week (with your daughter, of course—and the rest of your family too). If you don't belong to a church or synagogue, ask around and visit a congregation with a good reputation for helping people grow in their faith. We can and should pursue a personal and vibrant faith, but church is not just for marriages and baptisms and funerals; our spiritual life is meant to be lived in a community as well.

Week 7

THE PRIORITY OF LOVE

If I…know all mysteries and all knowledge;
and if I have all faith, so as to remove mountains,
but do not have love, I am nothing.
—1 Corinthians 13:2, NASB

In more than three decades of practicing medicine and being a parent, I've met fathers of every stripe. I've seen the disconnected ones who, partly out of guilt and partly out of ignorance, shower their daughters with expensive presents. I've seen others whose top priority is to make sure their girls enjoy great cultural and social advantages. I've interacted with some who drive their daughters relentlessly to excel academically or athletically ("It's for her own good," they're always quick to say). I've witnessed morally minded fathers withhold paternal approval whenever their daughters fail to act like "good girls" or violate family rules. And we've all seen the "wild and crazy" dads who seem like they're still living out their college fraternity days.

Heartbreaking are the comments of the thousands of girls and young women I've treated and visited with over the years. They consistently tell me they don't primarily want a gift-giving dad, a "sophisticated" dad, a success-minded dad, or a "cool, fun" dad. What they really want (and what they really need) is a father who loves them unconditionally.

This is the great legacy of my own father. He was a brilliant, introverted man. A successful pathologist, he was sometimes distracted. He missed many of my athletic events. He didn't talk much, and lots of times he also failed to listen well when I talked. So how did I know he loved me? As I have previously written of him, "I heard him worry about me to my mother. I watched him cry when my brother and I left home for college. . . . I knew he loved me because he made our entire family go on vacations together. Most of the time I hated going, particularly when I was a teen, but he made me go anyway. He knew something I didn't. He knew that we needed time to be together" (*Strong Fathers, Strong Daughters*, p. 3).

From a female perspective, may I offer four short reminders for dads about how to love your daughter?

Love is a commitment, not a feeling. Raising your daughter will involve plenty of magical and precious moments. At times your heart will swell with affection to the point that it feels like it just might break—just by watching your daughter. But true love is sacrificial, not sentimental.

A good father doesn't just show love when the mood strikes. He changes dirty diapers. He stays up with a sick kid to give his wife a break. He lays his hobbies aside for a season to spend more time with his kids. He is patient and kind and gentle, biting his tongue when he feels like uttering a stream of expletives. He even chases after the runaway teenage daughter who cursed him to his face and spit in his eye.

Love is heroic action, not just noble words. In the Bible, the apostle John urges people of faith: "Dear children, let's not merely say that we love each other; let us show the truth by our actions" (1 John 3:18, NLT).

Men are good at taking action, and strong fathers wake up daily with the determination to put their family first, knowing that the essence of life-changing love is selflessness, of making sacrifices, even small ones, that put others ahead of oneself. As the former Chicago Bears running back Gale Sayers famously put it (quoting his track coach): "The Lord is first, my friends are second, and I am third."

Love is tough. Daughters know how to wrap dads around their little fingers.

Even strong, tough-as-nails men can become weak-kneed and wilt in the face of batted eyelashes, adorable smiles, and an ingratiating "Can I daddy?" But you need to stand your ground and speak your mind when your daughter tries to break your rules. King Solomon said it well: "Better is open rebuke than love that is concealed" (Proverbs 27:5, NASB).

This kind of tough love has to walk that fine line between firmness and harshness. Not correcting misbehavior is wrong. Saying yes to everything your daughter wants to do is wrong. Genuine love is tough, because, as the Bible reminds us, "Love does no wrong to others" (Romans 13:10, NLT), and frankly, fathers who are pushovers are not loving their daughters well.

Love is gracious. The apostle Paul expressed this better than anyone:

> Love is patient and kind. Love is not jealous or boastful or proud or rude. It does not demand its own way. It is not irritable, and it keeps no record of being wronged. It does not rejoice about injustice but rejoices whenever the truth wins out. Love never gives up, never loses faith, is always hopeful, and endures through every circumstance. (1 Corinthians 13:4–7, NLT)

No wonder Paul concluded in another place, "Let all that you do be done in love" (1 Corinthians 16:14, ESV).

Just as you need to walk the line between firmness and harshness, you need to walk the line between setting standards and picking nits. Think big, be gracious, focus on what really matters, focus on expressing your love in rules for your daughter that will benefit her in the future, because, as the author Willa Cather wrote, "where there is great love, there are always miracles."

What dad doesn't want the miraculous for his daughter—and for his relationship with her?

PRAY

God, when it comes to this topic of love, I've got a lot to learn. Forgive my failures to be selfless and sacrificial. Forgive the times I've avoided doing the loving thing because I didn't "feel like it." Please give me more of a Christ-like love for my daughter. Teach me how to love her when she's not acting very lovable. Help me to be tough but tender when love requires me to draw boundaries. Amen.

FLEX YOUR DAD MUSCLES

1. Spend a few minutes reading and meditating on 1 Corinthians 13, the famous "love chapter" of the Bible. What do you notice? What sticks out to you? Substitute your name for the noun "love" and see how accurately the passage reads.

2. If expressing your love verbally is hard for you, then do as the apostle John said (in the verse cited above). Love your daughter by *taking action*, by *doing* something for her good. Here are some ideas:

- Drive down a country road and pick wildflowers with her.

- Turn off your cell phone and play a board game with her.
- Take her out to eat and let her pick the restaurant.
- Play a game of cards with her.
- Remove the TV from her room and invite her instead to watch classic movies with you and your wife (your daughter might scoff, at first, at an old black and white Fred Astaire and Ginger Rogers flick...but she won't for long).
- Watch her dance or cheerleading routine and offer encouragement.
- Take her to feed the ducks.
- Take her to a movie and then go somewhere afterward to discuss it.
- Clear your schedule so that you can be at her next game or recital.
- Give her clear boundaries, spell out the consequences for crossing them, and give her literary examples to consider by starting a Dad-Daughter reading club. Here's a book she'll probably like, for you to start with, with contrasting heroines: *Gone with the Wind.*
- Cancel your Saturday plans and take a day trip with her someplace she wants to go.
- Volunteer to help coach her sports team.

- Instead of turning on the TV, help her with her homework.
- Help her do one of the chores she resists doing the most. Try to make the experience fun, and see if you can get her to laugh.
- Show her how to do something that she wants to learn to do and that you are good at (like playing guitar or hitting a golf ball).

3. Have a discussion with your wife. Evaluate ways in which your daughter has perhaps managed to "work you." Wrestle with these questions: Where do we need to tighten up? Where is a firmer and tougher version of love needed?

THE PRIORITY OF INTEGRITY

*People with integrity walk safely, but those who
follow crooked paths will be exposed.*
—Proverbs 10:9, NLT

The best dads, the strongest fathers, are men of integrity—upright and trustworthy. When engineers say a bridge has "integrity," they mean that it is sound and solid, a unified whole. So too, men with integrity embody their values; their private lives and their public lives are in alignment. As the old saying goes, character is what you do when no one is watching.

In his letter to Titus, a first-century pastor, the apostle Paul wrote about the importance of integrity. "In everything," Paul urged, "set them an example by doing what is good. In your teaching show integrity" (Titus 2:7, NIV).

That's a great challenge, and not just for church leaders. It applies to everyone—especially fathers who are asked to set an example to their children "by doing what is good" in "everything." Dr. Ken Boa has written on this very point, noting that "Perhaps a good word to describe this trait of integrity is 'consistency.' There must be consistency between what is inside and what is outside" (Ken Boa, *The Perfect Leader: Practicing the Leadership Traits of God*, Colorado Springs: David C. Cook, 2006, p. 14). In other words, your talk and your actions need to be in sync.

In *Strong Fathers, Strong Daughters*, I challenged dads to imagine walking their daughter down the aisle on her wedding day. I wrote that "the man you see at the other end of the aisle will undoubtedly be a reflection of you—be that good or bad. It's the way it is: women are drawn to what they know" (p. 151).

Of all the arguments to be a man of integrity, that might be the clincher for the father who cares about his daughter. Daughters watch their dads. Your little girl (or teenage girl) studies you and notices what you say and do. This is why you can't afford to live a double life. You can't cut corners. You can't engage in secret behaviors that you're forever trying to cover up, because eventually she'll know; and when suitors come calling, she will be willing to settle for a man without high character.

Let me be quick to point out that having integrity doesn't mean being perfect. Nobody is 100 percent consistent. But having integrity does mean taking responsibility for mistakes, failures, and wrong choices. It means humbly acknowledging exactly where you fell short, apologizing for offenses, seeking forgiveness, and working to rebuild trust.

To recognize a good man, your daughter has to know one; so *be* her example of integrity. Set the bar high, be honest and be whole.

Here's the encouraging truth: if you are authentic, your daughter will have a great model of masculinity. But if you aren't, be prepared; for your daughter, your actions will speak louder than your words.

Make the commitment to inspire trust and respect in your daughter. Determine to integrate your faith and moral values into every facet of your life. Resolve to be a man of integrity.

PRAY

God, I don't want to be a hypocrite. I don't want to give my daughter the wrong picture of what a man is. Grant me wisdom and courage as I seek to align what I know is right with the way I live my life. Amen.

FLEX YOUR DAD MUSCLES

Here are two concrete ways you can cultivate integrity this week:

First, as you think through the content of this chapter, consider if you need to go to your daughter (or your wife or someone else) and seek forgiveness. Maybe you broke a promise. Or maybe she saw you get really angry and blow your top—when you've been preaching self-control to her. Humble yourself and make amends.

Second, schedule some time to sit down with a good friend, or with a small discussion group, or with a clergyman and talk through the idea of integrity. One book that some men's reading groups have found inspiring and helpful on the topic is *Robert*

E. Lee on Leadership: Executive Lessons in Character, Courage, and Vision, by H. W. Crocker III.

Week 9

THE PRIORITY OF EXAMPLE

Follow my example, as I follow the example of Christ.
—1 Corinthians 11:1, NIV

C hildren need to see things. They need words, yes, but even more than that they need experience. It's not enough to explain to your six-year-old how to clean her goldfish bowl. She needs to watch you do it, probably a few times, and then help you do it, before she tackles the task herself.

Remember the old adage:

I hear, I forget.
I see, I remember.
I do, I understand.

Strong fathers grasp this truth. They embrace the importance of action, experience, and being a role model.

At the end of his life, the apostle Paul wrote to his young protégé: "But you, Timothy, certainly know what I teach, and how I live, and what my purpose in life is. You know my faith, my patience, my love, and my

45

endurance. You know how much persecution and suffering I have endured" (2 Timothy 3:10–11, NLT). Note Paul's emphasis on his faith as it has been lived not just spoken (though both are mentioned and important).

For strong fathers, it comes down to this: if you want your daughter to be hardworking, then be a conscientious worker and use everyday activities—like washing the car or sweeping the kitchen—as implicit lessons in getting things done and not being sloppy or slothful.

Want to raise a compassionate kid? Let her see your kindness and concern for friends and neighbors who are hurting. Take her with you to visit a friend in the hospital or a grandparent in the nursing home.

Would you like your daughter to be honest? Then be honest yourself and value honesty in your interactions with others.

Want her to be courageous (and to value brave, cool-headed men when she's dating)? Then be strong and bold in the face of trouble.

Your daughter learns how to solve problems by seeing you solve problems. You give her a graduate course in grit by hanging in there yourself when times are tough. You teach her about the importance of sexual purity by avoiding TV shows and movies that make light of adultery or promiscuity.

You give her the best example of the importance of faith when you trust God and rely openly on prayer. When you genuinely love God, your daughter will too. This is because our children—especially when they are small—are little mimics. They copy our behavior and emulate our character. We create an expectation for them of what is right and normal, what is good and bad.

In every area of life, the actions you take will have a more profound impact on your daughter than the words you speak, as important as those words are. One genuine, simple act of humility—sincerely apologizing after a spat, or stooping to do a nasty, menial task without complaining—will teach your daughter more about humility than a hundred "mini-sermons" on the topic.

What are you showing your daughter? A strong father is mindful of little eyes watching, little ears listening, little minds learning about the values of hard work, compassion, and charity, of humility, prudence, and chastity. How you live your life will have an enormous influence on how your daughter lives hers. That's something that every father should always remember.

PRAY

God, I am struck by the powerful influence I have on my daughter. How easily I forget this sobering responsibility. How quickly I lose sight of this privilege: the blessing of being a father. If I'm honest, I know I haven't always been the best role model. I ask for Your grace and forgiveness and I ask that You please give me the wisdom and strength I need to be a better father. Amen.

FLEX YOUR DAD MUSCLES

Spend an hour doing something with your daughter. It doesn't really matter what you choose to do. You may choose to do a chore together, help her with homework, read to her, walk around the block, play catch, run errands, let her practice driving, or hit tennis balls.

As you are with her, things will happen. Life will occur. You will have to make choices.

IF...	YOU CAN EITHER EXHIBIT...	OR YOU CAN SHOW...
She is chatty	Interest	Boredom
She bursts into tears	Compassion and tenderness	Indifference
Traffic backs up	Patience	Impatience
She is snippy and moody	Love and understanding	Irritation
She is extremely silly and playful	Spontaneity	Frustration
She expresses a desire to quit	Encouragement	Scorn
She confesses something big	Grace and acceptance	Shock and disapproval
She wrecks the car	Gentleness	Anger
It's been a bad day	Trust in God	Anxiety

The main thing is to cultivate the habit of consciously remembering that at any given moment your daughter is watching how you react.

Be careful. Pray constantly for help. You won't do it perfectly, but keep working at it. If you blow it, lean into God's grace and try again.

The Priority of Forethought

*Careful planning puts you ahead in the long run;
hurry and scurry puts you further behind.*
—Proverbs 21:5, MSG

One of the worst things you can do as a father—and it is an epidemic among parents these days—is simply *react* to what your children do. Sure, children look to see how their parents react—but strong fathers don't just react, they lead, and leading requires a plan.

A strong father is a smart father who knows, in the words of the old adage, that an ounce of prevention is worth a pound of cure. When girls get into trouble, it's almost inevitably the case that their fathers were insufficiently involved in their lives and didn't provide them with the guidance and examples these girls needed.

And it's not as though these fathers didn't have good hearts and intentions. They loved their daughters deeply. But their priorities were misplaced. At work, they could be bold and decisive, but at home, rather than being models of leadership and strength, they could be surprisingly passive.

I suspect there are many reasons for this widespread passivity. Many dads are simply exhausted after a stressful workday. At home in their "castles," they just want to go off duty.

And they can justify this to themselves by saying: "Part of growing up is learning to find your own way; my daughter's smart and capable; and anyway, if she *really* needs me, I'll be here."

The problem is, by the time she "really" needs you it could be too late.

It's true that you can't plan every aspect of your daughter's life, but a little forethought goes a long way. The Book of Proverbs offers this instruction to plan ahead: "Ants—they aren't strong, but they store up food all summer" (Proverbs 30:25 NLT).

Christ, at a crucial point in His ministry, told His followers to be prepared: "Get ready for trouble. Look to what you'll need; there are difficult times ahead" (Luke 22:36, MSG).

Few of us simply drift through life—or if we do, we end up learning that it's a mistake—because we know we need to make plans, set priorities, and be prepared for the future.

We think, for example, often and carefully about retirement; some of us huddle with a financial advisor at least annually. We take our cars in for regular maintenance, and certainly before a big road trip. We visit the dentist at least once a year, if not twice, for routine exams. Hunters spend months leading up to hunting season checking their stands, blinds, and camps. They sight in their rifles and familiarize themselves with new wildlife regulations.

Smart fathers bring that same sense of preparedness, of forethought, of action to the raising of their daughters. Just as you learned when she started crawling and taking her first steps to "baby proof" your house, to prevent her from hurting herself, your daughter still needs the benefit of your experience as she grows up. Don't keep the light of your wisdom hidden under a bushel because of fatigue ("I'm too tired to do anything but watch TV") or fear ("I don't know how to talk to my daughter"); she needs your direction. And you can't give her direction unless you have a plan. So make one.

A few tips:

Be aware. Be aware of your daughter's stage of life, her needs, her weaknesses and strengths. Think about where she's going—the trajectory of her life if current trends continue. And don't leave yourself out of this assessment: Is the trajectory of your life as a father one of passivity, working hard at the office, but parking in front of the television at home? Or are you giving your daughter the advice, guidance, interaction, and leadership she needs?

Make a plan. Huddle with your wife. Share your thoughts, about where your daughter is, where you want her to be, and how you can help her get there. Pray together for wisdom.

If you don't have a coherent and clear plan, you can use The 12 Principles of Raising Great Kids from The Strong Parent Project online program. This practical resource takes a step-by-step approach, focusing on twelve principles that any father can learn. Whether your daughter is two or twenty this plan *works.*

Maybe for now your plan can be as simple as finding ways to spend more time *daily* with your daughter (one easy way: read to her before bedtime; even when she's older, you could read psalms or proverbs before nightly prayers). Make sure your plan is flexible, because we all know life happens. But as much as you can, make a plan, make it work, and stick to it.

Take action. With a clear sense of where you are and where you want to go, you assert yourself. Being a parent is about *raising* your child. That's your responsibility, your duty, and dads who shirk it are the ones who often end up shaking their heads and asking, "How did this happen?" It probably happened because of inadvertent neglect.

I love what my friends at Authentic Manhood say: "Real men reject passivity, accept responsibility, lead courageously, and invest eternally."

Be that kind of man. Be a man who plans, who thinks ahead, who is prepared—be a man of forethought, it's part of being a father.

Pray

God, I confess that I have been passive, that I have checked out, at times, when my daughter needs me, that I have failed to lead, and that I have not properly planned for my daughter's future. I ask that You strengthen me in courage and wisdom for this divinely appointed task of fathers. Amen.

Flex Your Dad Muscles

There is a course I wish every man and father could take. It's called *33: The Series*, and it's a six-volume DVD series produced by Authentic Manhood. You can find out more and see sample clips at www.authenticmanhood.com.

It offers practical biblical insights on God's design for men and fathers. Tens of thousands of participants have found the material life-changing, refreshing, and inspiring. I suspect you will too.

Week 11

THE PRIORITY OF PEACE

Blessed are the peacemakers, for they
will be called children of God.
—Matthew 5:9, NIV

Conflict upsets us, but it shouldn't surprise us. Wherever there are people—husbands and wives, dads and daughters—there will always be tension. How could it be otherwise? In any given situation, individuals have different ways of seeing things, different desires, and different agendas. Our interactions are filled with miscommunication and misunderstanding. All too often we are guilty of not communicating or not listening.

Experience shows us that the three most typical human responses to conflict are fleeing, fighting, or freezing. Some people check out at the first inkling of trouble. They escape, either physically retreating or emotionally withdrawing. Others go on the attack, seeing conflict as a personal affront, even a take-no-prisoners battle to be won. Still others, when emotions get high, become paralyzed. Not sure of what to do, they do nothing. Of course, none of these approaches solves the problem at hand. All exacerbate or prolong it.

Even though conflict is a fact of life, it doesn't have to consume our lives. Smart fathers realize their daughters look to them to be peacemakers in their lives and homes.

The Hebrew word for *peace* is *shalom*. It is an unbelievably rich word with a wide range of connotations. Depending on the context, it can mean "wholeness," "health," "security," or "prosperity." It describes a state of blessing, vitality, community, and harmony.

The longer we ponder God's idea of *shalom*, the more it becomes clear that we were meant to experience more than just the *absence* of visible tension and conflict. God also wants us to know the *presence* of deep wholeness and joy, of peace and spiritual prosperity, of *shalom*.

How does that happen? How do you become a man whose home is a place of peace? Make these commitments:

Commit to address, not avoid, tension. Don't ignore the proverbial elephant in the room. Don't leave the scene. Have the courage to lean into conflict. When you stand tall in the midst of conflict, it shows your daughter you care enough to listen to her and protect her.

Commit to engage in a healthy and constructive manner. Verbal "fights" can often be destructive. Sadly, we're all too familiar with that. There is, however, another way to work through conflict that *is* constructive and can actually lead to a richer, better relationship with your daughter. Here are some tips:

- *Stop.* Ask yourself: *Am I too emotional right now to have a rational, calm discussion?* If so, declare a brief time-out, but set a time when you and your daughter will talk. Never allow conflict to go unaddressed overnight.
- *Seek God's help.* Always ask for divine wisdom (and an extra measure of gentleness and patience) before you begin talking through volatile issues.
- *Search your own heart.* Be humble enough to own any wrong attitudes or actions you contributed to the disagreement at hand.

- *Strive to restore the relationship.* The goal is never to win an argument or be "right." The goal is to win the heart of your daughter and to be reconciled. That's being a peacemaker.
- *Speak peaceful words.* Whatever you do, don't raise your voice. Shouting at your daughter to get her to obey is like trying to use the horn to steer your car. It doesn't work; in fact, it only intensifies tense situations. As I've noted on my blog, "Kids who are yelled at by their parents are more likely to have depression and behavior problems.... Words cut deeply—particularly the words that flow from a parent's mouth to a child—whether that child is 6 or 66.... Some parenting experts say that kids don't hear parents scream because they tune them out. I completely disagree. Kids hear all right; they just pretend not to hear because they simply don't know what to do with the hurt."

Commit to truth telling. Don't pursue peace at any cost. Biting your tongue may seem like the easy way to harmony, but clamming up when you really need to speak leads to long-term pain. In *Strong Fathers, Strong Daughters*, I tell the story of Alicia, who was swept off her feet by an older man named Jack. When Alicia's father first met Jack, all his buzzers went off. His protective instincts kicked in. Something wasn't right about his daughter's suitor. The concerned father soon confronted his daughter gently but firmly, asking her not to go through with her plans for marriage. This infuriated Alicia so much she asked her dad to leave her apartment. Then just two weeks before the wedding, the truth about Jack came out—he had three wives and a criminal past. Guess whom Alicia called first? Her brave father, who had lovingly confronted her about her plans.

Together the two of them went to confront Jack. Alicia broke off the engagement and was spared a world of heartache. How easy it would have been for Alicia's father to look the other way. But strong dads don't do that. They don't run from uncomfortable situations. They engage. They speak up. Don't be a father who capitulates to his daughter just so she won't make a big scene or stop talking to you. Peacemakers boldly speak the truth in love.

Commit the outcome to God. It takes two parties to have true peace. You can make overtures, you can offer olive branches, but you cannot make your daughter (or anyone else) like the truth you feel led to say. No amount of effort on your part can guarantee your daughter will bury the hatchet and enter into a restored, harmonious relationship. This is why the apostle Paul counseled, "If it is possible, as far as it depends on you, live at peace with everyone" (Romans 12:18, NIV). "If it is possible, as far as it depends on you" means you can only do your part. All you can do is, literally, all you can do. Commit to be a bold and gentle truth teller and peacemaker; then trust God for the rest.

PRAY

God, since conflict is a regular part of life, I need to become more skilled at resolving it. I want to be a peacemaker. I want Your peace, *shalom*, in my life and in my relationships at home—especially with my daughter. Give me wisdom and self-control so that my conflicts become constructive and not destructive. Amen.

FLEX YOUR DAD MUSCLES

Look over the principles for peacemaking in this chapter one more time. Then take your daughter for ice cream or coffee and share them with her. Ask her how well she thinks you and your family live out these guidelines. (Note: Don't get defensive if she responds with some uncomfortable truth.) Then, if you have a recent unresolved conflict between the two of you, acknowledge the "elephant in the ice-cream/coffee shop." Have a thoughtful, respectful, constructive discussion about the situation.

THE VIRTUES OF STRONG FATHERS

Week 19: Gentleness

Week 20: Grit

Week 21: Honesty

Week 22: Humility

Week 23: Joy

Week 24: Patience

Week 25: Purity

Week 26: Self-Control

Week 12

COMPASSION

Just as a father has compassion on his children,
so the Lord has compassion on those who fear Him.
—Psalms 103:13, NASB

I never imagined that my work as a pediatrician would lead me to consult with players in the National Football League about how to be better fathers.

When I was first approached about this position, I politely declined. What did I have to tell pro football players? The last thing they needed or wanted, I assumed, was a grandmother pediatrician. *They would relate better to a man*, I thought, *preferably an ex-athlete who understands their unique world.*

I was wrong. Most of the players with whom I have consulted in the NFL Fatherhood Initiative relate extremely well to older women. This is because so many of them grew up interacting mostly with moms, grandmothers, and aunts. They never had a father figure in their early lives (even though they desperately longed for a father's attention).

Initially I interviewed some twenty players. Overwhelmingly, they expressed inner turmoil and insecurity about their own calling as fathers. This was due, in large part, to their not having had an example in their own lives of how to be a good father. They had no clue about how a father is supposed to act in the home. These men were also marked by enormous pain that they carried from their own childhoods—what my friends at Authentic Manhood would call a "father wound." Many choked up as they talked about the fathers they never knew.

I mention all this simply to say I don't think most dads grasp the life-changing impact their very existence has on their children. Present or absent, attentive or inattentive, compassionate or cruel, you *will* mark your daughter. One way or another, you *will* make an indelible imprint on her life. And I know your heart's desire is to be a father who honors God and blesses his child.

For a few moments, let's explore how you can have a positive impact on her life through the virtue of *compassion*.

In the Scripture verse at the beginning of this chapter, what does the psalmist mean when he speaks of a father's *compassion* or God's *compassion*? The Hebrew word is *racham*. It's a beautiful term. It is sometimes translated as "pity" or "mercy." In essence, to have compassion on another person is to show kindness and concern for that individual when they are in difficulty, whether or not the person deserves your help. Interestingly, a related Hebrew word is translated "womb" (some believe this is meant to suggest the deep affection and concern a mother has for her unborn child) or "bowels" (perhaps to bring to mind the way we feel punched in the gut or sick to our stomachs when we see others suffer).

What are some ways a dad can cultivate such compassion?

Empathize. Think back over your own childhood and teenage years. Remember what it felt like to have braces; move to a new place; lose a pet; feel uncoordinated or gangly or clumsy or ugly or awkward; get acne; not make the team; have a friend betray you; have a girlfriend break up with you; miss a free throw that would have tied the game and sent it into over-time; do badly on the test that you actually did study for; not get into the college of your choice. Tap into those memories; it will give you a newfound compassion for the things your daughter is facing.

Examine. Do a study of the life of Christ. Read the Gospel of Mark (the action-oriented life of Christ). As you do, you'll discover no one ever had compassion like Christ. Here are just three snapshots of His compassionate nature:

- "Moved with compassion, Jesus reached out and touched him. 'I am willing,' he said. 'Be healed!' Instantly the leprosy disappeared, and the man was healed" (Mark 1:41–42, NLT).
- "Jesus saw the huge crowd as he stepped from the boat, and he had compassion on them because they were like sheep without a shepherd" (Mark 6:34, NLT).
- "I have compassion for these people; they have already been with me three days and have nothing to eat" (Mark 8:2, NIV).

You'll notice in every case, Jesus' compassion didn't stop with mere feelings of sympathy. His tender mercy included a willingness to step boldly into the lives of those who were hurting—no e-mails or "likes" on Facebook, but face-to-face love and help. Can you imagine the power of a dad who is not only present in his daughter's life but also marked by this kind of gentle Christ-like compassion and mercy in all his dealings with his daughter?

Engage. Every day you'll get new opportunities to cultivate and demonstrate compassion. Here are some specific situations in which you can shine:

- Be patient with her (not frustrated with her) when she is terrified of the dark.
- Be sad with her when she is sad. "Be happy with those who are happy, and weep with those who weep" (Romans 12:15, NLT).

- Get down on the ground with her when she has fallen and hurt herself.
- Pay attention to her when she is nervously talking about a situation in her life (even if you think it's trivial).
- Hold her when she says things like "I'm ugly" or "None of the boys like me" or "All my friends make fun of me."
- Comfort her when she has failed to accomplish a goal.
- Resist the urge to criticize when she misses the easy basket or strikes out in the big game.

As a father, you are your daughter's first and most important experience of male love, compassion, and kindness (or indifference, anger, and cruelty). Whatever your early interactions with her, they will be imprinted deeply on her brain and heart. For the rest of her life, every experience she has with a male will be filtered through her experiences with you. The good news is that if she trusts you from an early age, she will be more likely to seek out trustworthy men. If she has been hurt by you, she will shy away—even disengage—from men. Don't let that happen.

If you've failed in this area, do not despair. I have seen many fathers, stepfathers, and grandfathers turn a girl's life around with a renewed commitment to demonstrate love, show compassion, and give attention.

As your daughter navigates her way through an often harsh world, may she be able to say from the depths of her heart, "Because of the LORD's great love we are not consumed, for his compassions never fail" (Lamentations 3:22, NIV). And as she reflects on God's great love and compassion, may your love and compassion come to her mind as well.

Pray

God, I am so grateful for Your compassion in my life. When I deserved nothing from You, You blessed me more than I can ever say. I ask that Your compassion might flow through me to my daughter. Help me mark her life in eternally good ways. Amen.

Flex Your Dad Muscles

Teach your daughter the importance of compassion—and model it for her—by finding someone in your church, neighborhood, or community who is facing a financial or medical crisis. Together, deliver a meal; or take them some cash (in an envelope) and leave it secretly in a safe place where only they will be sure to find it.

Week 13

CONTENTMENT

I have learned to be content whatever the circumstances.
—Philippians 4:11, NIV

In *Strong Fathers, Strong Daughters*, I wrote about a pernicious problem that has invaded most North American homes: material discontent. "Men, of course, are trained from the day they enter school to be career-oriented, and most men measure their career success and even their happiness in terms of money. We all like to believe that having more will make us happier. So many men think in terms of gain: material things, career advancement, a bigger bank account, a prettier wife. But the constant pursuit of more never leads to happiness; it only leads to dissatisfaction with what we have" (p. 164).

Why are we so susceptible to marketers and advertisers? How is it that we get sucked in by those silly infomercials? What is the deep magic that overcomes us when we walk into a store intending only to look around yet walk out with a couple of bags and several hundred dollars in new charges to our credit card? When will we ever learn that the constant pursuit of *more* leads not to satisfaction but to perpetual dissatisfaction?

In my life and in my work I have come to see that one of the most important virtues among strong fathers is the character trait of *contentment*. Consider what the Scripture says:

> For we brought nothing into the world, and we can take nothing out of it. But if we have food and clothing, we will be content with that. Those who want to get rich fall into temptation and a trap and into many foolish and harmful desires that plunge people into ruin and destruction. For the love of money is a root of all kinds of evil. Some people, eager for money, have wandered from the faith and pierced themselves with many griefs. (1 Timothy 6:7–10, NIV)

Notice the apostle Paul doesn't single out money per se as the issue. No, it's "the love of money" that is the problem. Paul insists here that the desire for money in order "to get rich" is how and where we start moving into dangerous territory. What other motives would drive so many men to invest in questionable, get-rich-quick schemes? Why else would so many fathers gamble away a hard-earned paycheck on a Friday night at the casino? When we consider our insatiable appetite for "more," it's no wonder so many men live with the grief of debt or the pressure of having to work an extra job (or two).

Elsewhere in the New Testament, we find this concise command: "Keep your life free from love of money, and be content with what you have" (Hebrews 13:5, ESV).

It's worth pointing out that the Greek verb translated *be content* in both these passages means "to be sufficient" or "to be adequate." In other words, the contented man focuses on what he has and says, "This is sufficient. I have *enough*." He peacefully enjoys whatever blessings God has given.

The discontented man, on the other hand, stares longingly at all the things he doesn't possess. "I want that…and that…and that…I just want *more*." He then restlessly schemes and scrambles about how to get those desired things. Someone once asked John D. Rockefeller, at one point the world's richest man: "How much money is enough?" His answer: "Just a little bit more."

As a dad, it might be a good time to examine your own heart. How contented are you? Do you constantly think about ways to make more money? Do you daydream about ways to acquire more stuff? Do you bad-mouth your existing possessions—your "small" house, your "old, beat-up" car, your "ratty" furniture? Do you talk incessantly about the trips you wish you were on or the gadgets you wish you had?

If your daughter sees you constantly striving for more—rather than working hard for the sake of doing a good job—she will slowly absorb the unhealthy idea that "more" is better, that "more" equals happiness. By your own actions you will be teaching her that fulfillment in life is contingent on a bigger house, a better vacation, and a higher income. You will be training her to be discontented with all that she currently has. She will consciously or unconsciously buy the lie that it takes a steady stream of newer vehicles, cooler gadgets, and other marks of the "good life" (expensive jewelry, the newest fashions) in order to be content.

Here's what I know to be a fact: contentment will *never* come if we are continually looking outward at the next thing we want to get.

So how do we cultivate contentment? The first step is to realize that most of the things we say we "need" are really wants. If we can both see that and say that, then we can subject those desires to the priorities we've previously set for our lives. We can ask questions like these: *What matters most in the end—people or things? What if I spend my life trying to accumulate this stuff but in the process I lose my family and warp my soul?*

Contentment comes with being satisfied with what we have right now. A father who lives his life with the mind-set of "more is not the answer" and "enough is enough" will teach his daughter an important lesson about life's priorities. The father who doesn't reconcile his wants and desires with honesty, integrity, and humility will likely raise a daughter who is greedy. More than likely, she will marry a discontented man.

Don't look for contentment in a job, in your bank account, online, or at the mall. Look close to home for contentment. Appreciate what is right there in front of you. If this is a major struggle for you, maybe you'd benefit from taking the "Anti-Stuff Challenge." That's where you decide not to buy anything new (other than food and personal care items, of course) for one week, one month, or maybe even six months. The experience will change you, and I guarantee it will cause you to feel happier.

PRAY

God, forgive me for the times I am more dissatisfied than thankful. You have given me so much. I want to learn to focus on all I have, not on the things I don't have. Not only that, but I want to set a good example of contentment for my daughter. I want her to learn that You always meet our needs, and many times You give us way more than we really need. Amen.

FLEX YOUR DAD MUSCLES

To give you a perspective on how much you actually do have compared to most people in the world, go to http://www.

globalrichlist.com. There, in a matter of seconds, you can see how much better off you are than you might think.

Go for a walk with your daughter and take turns talking about all the things you are thankful for. Enumerating and expressing gratitude to God helps us cultivate a contented spirit. It gets us focusing on all the blessings we possess instead of all the things we don't have.

Week 14

COURAGE

Be strong and courageous, for you are the one who will lead
these people to possess all the land I swore to their ancestors
I would give them. Be strong and very courageous.
—Joshua 1:6–7, NLT

Most people remember where they were on September 11, 2001. The memories of the 9/11 attacks are forever etched into the American psyche: nineteen radical Islamic terrorists, four hijacked commercial jetliners, nearly three thousand deaths, over six thousand injuries, and a cost to the United States—according to a *New York Times* estimate—of some $3.3 trillion.

It was a catastrophic day. And yet not everything about 9/11 was ugly and awful. All during those dark hours there were flashes of remarkable courage.

I still shake my head in awe and get goose bumps when I watch the surreal footage of that day. Videos show police and firefighters running *into* the Twin Towers to rescue those trapped inside as the masses fled the burning buildings. Even after the collapse of the first tower, those brave men and women continued their search, costing more than four hundred of them their lives.

It was more of the same on Flight 93. A small band of ordinary passengers realized their need to take immediate action. Bravely storming the cockpit, they overpowered the hijackers, keeping them from carrying out plans to steer that plane into either the Capitol or the White House.

Thankfully, most of us will never be presented with those kinds of dramatic life-and-death choices. And yet, not a day goes by that we don't face at least one stressful or anxious situation, maybe even a few moments of outright fear.

What we need most in such moments is courage. Eddie Rickenbacker, Medal of Honor recipient for his daring exploits as a World War I ace pilot, put it best: "Courage is doing what you are afraid to do. There can be no courage unless you're scared."

Every good father can relate to that statement. Honest dads will tell you that having a daughter is unnerving—even on the best days, because you're always on the alert to protect your daughter. My point is simply this: dads of daughters need lots and lots of courage.

Sadly, too many moms and dads act out of fear, not faith and strength. They are fearful their kids will rebel or not like them, possibly even leave them. So they compromise, back down, and avoid confrontation. That's not playing defense, which you sometimes have to do; it's abdicating responsibility. Irresponsibility never leads to joy, only to eventual trouble and heartache.

Where does a man find the will, the determination, and the guts to do all the daunting things necessary to raise a strong daughter? Consider the situation of Joshua. Put yourself in his place for a few moments.

It's around 1400 BC. The scene is the plain of Moab adjacent to the banks of the Jordan River, just east of the Promised Land. The twelve ragtag tribes of Israel—several million men, women, and children—are gathered to hear the great Moses speak his final words of challenge. The revered lawgiver reminds the people of their checkered history. He urges them to remain faithful to God. Then he turns to Joshua, his handpicked successor. The mantle of leadership is about to fall on him. It will be Joshua's responsibility to lead this headstrong, fickle bunch into the land. Pay close attention to Moses's charge: "So be strong and courageous! Do not be afraid and do not panic before them. For the LORD your God will personally go ahead of you. He will neither fail you nor abandon you" (Deuteronomy 31:6, NLT).

According to Moses, the object of Joshua's panic and fear is the pronoun "them." By "them" Moses probably meant the enemies of Israel in the Promised Land. And "them" also could have referred to the rebellious Israelites themselves. Whatever the case, when Joshua found himself before "them," feeling afraid, what was he to do? Be *courageous*. This rich Hebrew word means "to be strong, alert, brave, stout, bold, solid, hard." Where would Joshua get all those manly virtues? He would find them as he embraced the truth that God Almighty was continually with him. And he would exhibit them as he trusted that the God Who was *with* him would also faithfully *help* him.

What a great reminder for fathers of daughters. "Them" could be boys who want to use your pretty, innocent daughter for sexual gratification. "Them" might be peers whose approval currently means the world to your daughter. "Them" are the dangerous cultural values that seem to be capturing her heart, mind, and will. "Them" are fellow parents who roll their eyes at the strict boundaries you've set for your daughter. "Them" could be the many changing moods of your daughter. Or "them" could be all the conflicting voices and competing questions in your own head.

The point is, when you feel uncertainty and tension, or even panic and fear before "them"—whatever "them" is—you can find in the promise and presence and power of God the necessary courage to do what needs to be done.

The list of things a father is called to bravely confront is long and daunting. Your daughter needs you to be prepared to do the following:

- Walk into an unchaperoned party of teens where the beer and booze is flowing and pull your daughter out.
- Take on a teacher who is belittling your child.
- Have uncomfortable, frank discussions with your daughter about sex (and about how guys think about sex).
- Weigh in on fashion choices—sometimes forbidding the wearing of certain outfits.
- Have a heart-to-heart with that new guy who is obviously interested in your daughter (and who bugs you in a way you can't quite articulate).
- Take away a smartphone.
- Explain to another parent why your daughter can't go with his or her daughter to a certain movie or concert.
- Unplug the TV or the Internet.

There will, of course, be consequences for all such actions. You might not be your daughter's favorite person for a period of time. But even bigger and graver consequences await the fathers who are unwilling to make those kinds of hard decisions.

As I wrote in *Strong Fathers, Strong Daughters*, "Have courage under fire. Yes, you will be fired upon—by friends, pop psychologists, television programs, your wife, and your daughter. Keep your cool, but be firm and consistent. In the best men, kindness, strength, and perseverance go together" (p. 47).

In a day when so many girls are in serious trouble and so many fathers are distracted or afraid to act, we need a new generation of courageous men. Your daughter needs a dad who will engage, a dad who will not be paralyzed by fear but who will run *toward* the trouble.

In his inaugural address in 1905, Teddy Roosevelt said these stirring words, which are applicable to the task of fathering: "We must show, not merely in great crises, but in the everyday affairs of life, the qualities of practical intelligence, of courage, of hardihood, and endurance."

God will give you those qualities if you ask Him.

PRAY

God, when I feel fear, it's a reminder that I need to call on You for courage. Thank You for the promise that You are with me. Thank You for the assurance of divine help. I pray that You might grant me the confidence and wisdom I need to raise a strong, courageous daughter. Amen.

FLEX YOUR DAD MUSCLES

After a minute of honest reflection, write down a list of what makes you tense, nervous, anxious, or afraid. Here's a list of fears common among fathers:

- Standing alone against the parenting crowd. (What if all the parents of my daughter's friends are saying "okay" but I think the answer in this situation needs to be "no way"?)
- Standing firm and enforcing agreed-upon rules. (What if she makes good on her threats to run away, harm herself, or make everyone else miserable?)
- Asking pointed, uncomfortable questions about her behavior. (What if she blows up and then clams up?)

Hearing painful, unwanted answers to my pointed questions. (What if I ask the scary question and she admits she's been abused or is sexually active or experimenting with drugs or alcohol?) Those are just a few examples. You probably have other paralyzing "what ifs." The point is to identify them. Then ask for the faith to act. Courage is taking a risk to do the right thing, even when your heart is pounding and your knees are shaky.

Week 15

CREATIVITY

*In the beginning God created the heavens
and the earth.... Then God said, "Let us make human
beings in our image, to be like us."*
—Genesis 1:1, 26, NLT

"Creative?" Tim snorts. "No way. That's the *last* thing in the world I am. I didn't get any of those genes in my family. My younger sister Karen—she's the creative one. You should hear her sing and play the piano. Back in high school she used to be in plays. Now she has a blog. And she's even writing a book. Me? I wouldn't know an adjective from an adverb. I'm a plumber. I fix leaky pipes and faucets. I unplug sewer lines and install toilets. Ha, I'm the complete opposite of creative."

Tim's thinking is reflective of most people's: creative = artsy. But that's a woefully incomplete understanding of creativity.

In the first sentence of the Bible we are introduced to God. Over the next few paragraphs God is described. But He's not presented there as God the Savior, or God the Supreme Being Who answers prayer, or God the Judge of the world. In fact, if the only information we had about God was what we read in Genesis 1 and 2, we would know one thing only about Him: He's the Almighty Creator. He creates. He is creative.

This is significant. Notice what happens as all this divine creative activity is moving toward a conclusion in Genesis 1. The triune God announces His intention: "Let us make human beings in our image, to be like us."

Theologians will tell you this phrase is loaded with meaning. But at the most basic level, it must mean God made people to be creative. Why? Because He is *the* Creator. And we were made to resemble Him. If we were designed to reflect His nature, and His nature is creative, then we must possess that quality as well.

And, of course, we do. Everyone is creative. Tim the plumber is. And his sister is. And you are too. Here is the miracle and mystery: God the Creator is infinitely creative—creative enough to make each person creative in wonderfully unique ways. Tim might not be able to write a blog post to save his soul, but you should see the ingenious plan he came up with just last month to move a bathroom down the hall in the renovation of an older home. Creativity applies to pipes as much as to poetry. Pediatricians need it (and have it) every bit as much as painters.

Here's why that matters in the realm of fatherhood. You are unique. There's never been a dad exactly like you. No one else has your exact perspective, background, experience, personality, or gifts.

The same can be said for your daughter. When God made her, He broke the proverbial mold. She's like an original Rembrandt. Logically, then, it follows that your relationship with her will be a true original. It won't look quite like any other father-daughter relationship. And it shouldn't.

Books (like *Strong Fathers, Strong Daughters*) and digital courses (like The 12 Principles of Raising Great Kids from The Strong Parent Project online program) can present broad wisdom about being a parent. But inevitably when it gets pressed down into your family it will look different than it does in some other family. And that's okay. Our creative God meant for it to be that way. The principles are universal; the application of those principles is unique.

So what are some ways your God-designed creativity should manifest itself in your role as a father? What does your daughter want and need from you in terms of creativity?

Creativity in teaching. A dad is a lot of things: provider, protector, leader, authority, fixer, and so on. One of his most important roles, however, is that of teacher. It is a father's responsibility to teach his daughter about God and about life. Moses put it this way to his people, "Listen, O Israel! The LORD is our God, the LORD alone. And you must love the LORD your God with all your heart, all your soul, and all your strength. And you must commit yourselves wholeheartedly to these commands that I am giving you today. Repeat them again and again to your children. Talk about them when you are at home and when you are on the road, when you are going to bed and when you are getting up" (Deuteronomy 6:4–7, NLT).

Good teachers will tell you there's no one-size-fits-all "secret" for teaching. Teaching requires creativity. Some kids are auditory learners. Others are visual. What works when a girl is six isn't always effective when she's sixteen. As you attempt to pass on important truths and crucial life lessons to your daughter, be creative. Study her unique personality, and tailor your teaching accordingly. Moses emphasized that dads will need to seize on every teachable moment in life. In other words, you have to be creative.

Creativity in having fun. If you have some beloved family traditions, by all means continue to practice and honor those. That's a hugely important part of building and shaping a family legacy. But be careful not to get stuck in a rut. Try new things with your daughter. Shared experiences are crucial for building a strong bond. Not only that, but stepping out of comfort zones builds confidence and a sense of adventure. You never know when a fun outing might lead to discovery of a new passion in her heart or an undiscovered, latent talent. For example, a Saturday outing to ride horses might just reveal your daughter's love for all things equestrian.

Creativity in getting your daughter to open up. Does she seem more relaxed when you're driving or sitting with you on a porch swing? Maybe it's when you're doing something together (such as raking leaves or playing ping-pong). Some kids are more chatty in the afternoon; others at bedtime. At one age, she might open up when you simply ask direct questions. But when she's older, she might respond better to brief anecdotes from your life. Creative dads try different things. If one strategy doesn't work, they concoct a new one.

Creativity in discipline. Every child has an Achilles' heel. There is something that they absolutely don't want to lose, and your job as a dad is to find it. What's the Kryptonite for your daughter? It might not be material. She might fear being taken from the soccer or dance team because it would embarrass her almost to death if you pulled her for bad behavior. Others might hate losing their iPad or smartphone privileges but wouldn't mind manual labor in the least. You have to be creative in figuring out what sort of consequences will work with your daughter. Use that to get her under control when she is out of control.

When we unleash and develop our creativity, it honors God by reflecting His nature to the world; it brings joy and blessings to ourselves and others. There's no satisfaction quite like having a "lightbulb" moment and devising a solution to a problem.

PRAY

Almighty God, I thank You for making me and making my daughter just the way we are. Show me how I can use my creativity to be a better father, to bring more joy into my house, and to have a better relationship with my daughter. Amen.

FLEX YOUR DAD MUSCLES

Make a list of five to twenty fun, creative experiences you'd like to do together. You might include some of the following ideas:

- Go scuba diving
- Learn to ride unicycles
- Start a business together
- Hike part of the Appalachian Trail
- Enter and run a 10K race together
- Write a book together
- Go to Alaska
- Learn to surf
- Write and record a song together

Be creative—don't settle for this meager list. Come up with your own. Then pick one project and begin working toward that together.

Week 16

FAITHFULNESS

Trust in the Lord and do good;
Dwell in the land and cultivate faithfulness.
—Psalms 37:3, NASB

I n *Strong Fathers, Strong Daughters*, I tell the story of Allison. She was a seventh-grader when her family moved. After a change of schools, Allison went into the proverbial tank. She started hanging out with the wrong crowd. This, in turn, led to drinking and smoking dope. An intervention by her family (with the demand that she enter an inpatient treatment program) only made things worse.

Allison's father, John, did something brilliant. Just before she was to be admitted to the program, he took his furious daughter camping on a remote island. (I think John chose the island so Allison wouldn't be able to run away.)

Not much happened during the weekend. They didn't talk much. They mostly hiked and read and made pancakes.

When they got home, Allison started her eight-month treatment program. Slowly she began to improve. Her depression lifted. Her anger dissipated. Through much of high school she and her father had a tenuous relationship. But by the time she turned eighteen, their relationship had completely turned around. In fact, by the end of Allison's college career, John's friends often spoke in envious terms of his relationship with his daughter.

Allison came by to see me, and I asked what had made such a difference in her life. Without missing a beat, she began talking about the infamous island camping trip with her father.

> I realized that weekend that he was unshakable. Sure, he was upset, but I saw that no matter what I did I could never push him out of my life. You can't believe how good that made me feel. Of course, I didn't want him to know that then. But that was it—the camping trip. I really think it saved my life. I was on a fast track to self-destruction. (*Strong Fathers, Strong Daughters*, p. 62)

I'm not suggesting here that camping is the panacea for all daddy-daughter tensions (though I've seen lots of good things come from such experiences). I am, however, advocating for more dads like John, unshakable dads who are *faithful* through all the ups and downs of being a parent.

The word translated *faithful* in the Hebrew Old Testament refers to someone who is loyal, reliable, steadfast, and worthy of trust. A faithful man is a man you can count on when the going gets rough.

A strong, faithful father is:

Faithful to God. He keeps the faith even (and especially) during the hard times. Like Job, a strong, faithful father should be ready to say, "Though he slay me, yet will I hope in him" (Job 13:15, NIV). We're not talking about *blind* faith, but about a quiet, settled faith that grows in understanding and is tenacious in its loyalty; as tenacious as your loyalty (and love) for your daughter.

Faithful to his wife. Strong, faithful fathers keep their wedding vows. There are few gifts you can give your daughter more important than the example of marital fidelity. Infidelity, as has been proven time and again, leads only to heartache and misery—not only for your spouse (and eventually for you) but devastatingly for your children.

Faithful to his children. Your daughter needs a rock, an anchor, and she looks for that in you. She needs you to be a person she can trust, who loves her unconditionally, and who will always be there for her—no matter what.

Faithful to friends. A strong, faithful father shows his daughter what faithful friendship looks like: patching up differences when necessary, helping out when friends are in trouble, enjoying fellowship—whether camping or at sporting events or in group Bible study. Especially as she enters adolescence, your daughter will see friendships destroyed by backstabbing and betrayal. She'll need an alternative model, a better model, and you should provide it.

In raising your daughter, trust the faithfulness of God, remember that "The steadfast love of the LORD never ceases; his mercies never come to an end; they are new every morning; great is your faithfulness" (Lamentations 3:22–23, ESV).

PRAY

God, I thank You for Your faithfulness and I pray that I might be as faithful to my daughter as You are to me. Amen.

Flex Your Dad Muscles

Make faithfulness a habit. Here are a few habits (consistent actions) that can strengthen your relationship with your daughter:

- Pray *for* her every day.
- Pray *with* her every day.
- Put her to bed every night you're home. Or if she's older, pop into her room every night at bedtime. Sit on her bed and visit for five minutes.
- Take her to school or pick her up from school every day (if your work schedule allows).
- Try to attend all her games or performances (don't beat yourself up if you miss some).
- Hug her when she's mad at you.
- Tell her you love her when she's most unlovable.
- Write her notes of encouragement on a regular basis.
- Put $5 or $15 or $25 or $50 a week (whatever you can afford) in a college savings fund for her.
- Let her see you reading the Bible every morning.
- Rave about your wife to your daughter—talk about all the reasons you love her.
- Let her see you staying in touch with old friends.

FORGIVENESS

*The Lord our God is merciful and forgiving,
even though we have rebelled against him.*
—Daniel 9:9, NIV

L ittle girls do little girl things. They accidentally spill red Kool-Aid all over your computer keyboard. They color flowers on every page of that business plan you were going to give to a potential investor today. What can you say? What can you do? She's just a kid, right? What does she know?

Then there are big girls. Big girls are capable of a lot more damage. And their actions are not always so "innocent." Take Natasha, for example. Abandoned as an infant, she spent most of her first fifteen years in Russia bouncing from orphanage to orphanage. As she neared the time of "aging out" ("graduation" from the orphanage into the real world—and, in all likelihood, into a life of prostitution), she was unexpectedly adopted by a God-fearing American couple from the Pacific Northwest.

Talk about an act of rescue! Suddenly, Natasha was part of a family. She had a home, loving parents, adoring siblings, a great school, and a devoted youth group at church. In truth, she got what few orphans ever get: a fresh start and real hope for the future. Everything seemed too good to be true.

Poor Natasha couldn't handle it all. She began stealing from her new parents and partying with a sketchy crowd. High on Ecstasy one night, she took her dad's car and flipped it, badly injuring the twenty-two-year-old pot dealer who was riding with her (also the father of the tiny baby growing inside her womb).

Natasha's adoptive father, Craig, is a good man. But he struggles with forgiving his daughter. "I don't understand. We have bent over backwards to give her a new life. I mean, we have *completely* disrupted our lives. We have loved Natasha with our whole hearts. How could she do all this? *Why* would she make such terrible choices?" Then, with his voice breaking, "I know I'm supposed to forgive. But, honestly, I don't trust her. Not even a little. I don't like all the drama she's brought into our home. Maybe this whole thing was just a big mistake?"

Wow. What would you tell Craig if he were a close friend?

Here's what God's Word says:

- "LORD, if you kept a record of our sins, who, O Lord, could ever survive? But you offer forgiveness, that we might learn to fear you"(Psalms 130:3–4, NLT).
- "Be kind and compassionate to one another, forgiving each other, just as in Christ God forgave you" (Ephesians 4:32, NIV).
- "Make allowance for each other's faults, and forgive anyone who offends you. Remember, the Lord forgave you, so you must forgive others" (Colossians 3:13, NLT).

It seems to me that the message of the Bible is twofold: (1) God completely forgives us in Christ. (2) Because we have been the recipients of such lavish mercy, we have to extend that same grace to others. We *have* to. Not forgiving others is not an option.

Here's the bottom line: girls make mistakes as they grow up. (We all do—bet you can remember plenty of boneheaded stunts you pulled as a kid. Am I right?)

A father's job is to teach his daughter what to do in moments of failure. When she makes bad choices, should she (a) deny her actions, (b) cover them up, or (c) blame someone else? The correct answer is (d) none of the above. She needs to learn to take responsibility for her failures, whether small or large.

In order for her to learn from her mistakes and to grow emotionally and spiritually in spite of them, your daughter has to do three things. First, she has to acknowledge her failure. Some girls have no problem with this; others really struggle. If your daughter doesn't like to admit when she's wrong, stay after her. This is not an optional life skill. It's mandatory. We don't need more adults who are "victims," who blame others for their own mistakes.

Second, she needs to apologize. Asking for God's forgiveness is primary—it demonstrates humility. (Ultimately, He's the One we sin against.) Then, saying "I'm sorry" to whomever she's hurt or offended is another essential discipline every girl needs to learn (and learn well).

Third, your daughter needs to put the incident behind her and move on (and you need to help her with this). This is the beauty and the power of the Christian gospel. Because of Jesus, we can have an unlimited number of fresh starts. God wipes away our offenses. The apostle John declared this good news: "If we confess our sins, he is faithful and just and will forgive us our sins and purify us from all unrighteousness" (1 John 1:9, NIV). That's a promise to tuck away—for both daughters and fathers.

One of the best ways you can help your daughter move forward is to demonstrate that *you* forgive her. Forgiveness is canceling the spiritual debt another person owes you. It doesn't mean you develop amnesia and no longer have any recollection of hurtful incidents. But it does mean you refuse to keep bringing those things up. You choose not to hold them against another person.

Show your daughter what forgiveness means. Give her a mulligan when she messes up. That's what God does for us.

PRAY

God, I thank You for your mercy and forgiveness, and I pray that I might demonstrate forgiveness to my daughter. Help me to forgive others as You have forgiven me. Amen.

FLEX YOUR DAD MUSCLES

Here's a fun project to do with your daughter. Order some Sulky Super Solvy—a sewing, embroidering, quilting material that dissolves "magically" in water.

Get your Solvy (you'll need a couple of pieces about 5" x 9"), a big bowl of warm water, a big wooden spoon, and a couple of markers. Talk to your daughter about God's forgiveness. Discuss with her what sin is—wrong acts, wrong thoughts, wrong talk that happen whenever we put our own sinful desires (envy, selfishness, boastfulness) ahead of how God wants us to live.

Tell your daughter, "Let's write a few of our sins from yesterday on our papers." (It's fine to write just four or five things.)

Explain that because God is holy and perfect, our sin separates us from Him. Explain that this is a BIG problem because we can't undo our sins. We can't erase them or pretend that we didn't commit them. Our need is for forgiveness. Our only hope is that God will forgive us for our sins.

Explain that this is why Jesus came. He came into the world in order to pay for our sins. In dying on the cross and rising from the grave, Jesus took our sins away and forgave them. All our sins. Forgiven forever. Read Hebrews 8:12: "For I will forgive their wickedness and *will remember their sins no more*" (NIV, emphasis added).

Have your daughter put her list of sins in the bowl and stir. Watch her face when her Solvy "sin list" dissolves before her eyes. Explain to her that because God forgives us fully and completely, we also are to forgive others.

Week 18

GENEROSITY

Remember the words of the Lord Jesus, that He Himself said,
"It is more blessed to give than to receive."
—Acts 20:35, NASB

A few years ago I read Daniel Day's book *Ten Days Without*. What an amazing account of one man's desire to make a difference. The book shook me up—in a really good way. Since reading it I don't think I've looked at shoes or coats the same.

Ten Days Without recounts Daniel's effort to provide shoes to needy children. To more closely identify with their plight, he decided to go without shoes himself for ten days. At the same time, he asked his friends to donate shoes for low-income children. Some time later, another thought hit him: *These kids don't have winter jackets either.*

So there in Colorado—in the middle of winter—Daniel began a second campaign to collect coats for kids. And yes, to raise awareness, he went ten days without a coat. He endured frigid weather, wearing only a long-sleeve shirt.

As I visited with Daniel about his experience, I was struck by his enthusiasm. His vivid descriptions of short-term misery were punctuated by this: "You will never take shoes for granted again when you stop at a gas station to use the men's room and you have no shoes on. And in the winter, when driving your kids to school without a coat, you come to appreciate the warmth you throw around your shoulders numerous times a day without a thought."

Going without shoes or jackets was only the beginning.

Daniel decided to make other temporary sacrifices: from giving up the ability to walk (his wife rolled him around in a wheelchair), to going mute, to giving up electronic media, to living without furniture.

These temporary sacrifices taught Daniel how rich he really was. It made him enormously grateful. It also deepened his desire to be more generous—and generosity is a key virtue of every strong father.

In Psalm 37, we read this observation of David: "The wicked borrow and do not repay, but the righteous give generously.... They are always generous and lend freely; their children will be a blessing" (Psalms 37:21, 26, NIV).

Notice the impact of a righteous man's generosity: his "children will be a blessing." In other words, if your children grow up seeing your generosity, they will be less self-centered and more generous themselves.

Proverbs 11:25, echoing the statement of Jesus (at the beginning of this chapter), speaks of the blessing that comes when we seek to bless others: "A generous person will prosper; whoever refreshes others will be refreshed" (NIV).

So how do we do it?

Here are some practical ways a dad can become more generous:

Time. This is your most precious possession. Are you available to your wife? To your daughter? Do you take time, *make* time, *carve out* time to be with the people you love? At dinner or during family times, are you always checking your watch or phone? Schedules aren't bad, but they can enslave us and make us miserly in the way we give time to others.

Wisdom and expertise. Since the day you were born, you've been learning lessons and important insights. Don't hoard this wisdom—share it. Tell your daughter about your successes and failures. Be generous in sharing your experience.

Spiritual truth. God's method for spreading the good news of His grace and love is simple. Those who have experienced it are to turn around and share it. The apostle Paul put it this way: "You have heard me teach things that have been confirmed by many reliable witnesses. Now teach these truths to other trustworthy people who will be able to pass them on to others" (2 Timothy 2:2, NLT).

Money and possessions. The Bible says that we really don't own anything. "The earth is the LORD's, and everything in it" (Psalms 24:1, NIV). In other words, everything belongs, ultimately, to God. This means we are simply stewards, or managers, of *God's* possessions, and we should constantly be asking ourselves what God wants us to do with our *temporary* ownership of them.

Affection. I plead with dads all the time not to be stingy with their physical affection. Hugs are almost magical in their ability to keep girls out of trouble. Often, a father pulls away from his daughter when she begins going through puberty—but that is entirely the wrong reaction. A dad needs to hug his teenage daughter more than ever. She needs hugs during this turbulent time, and all the research shows she'll do much better with them. Hug generously, dad.

Words of affirmation. It is so easy for parents to find fault with their kids. We see their flaws and we want to correct misbehavior. There's surely nothing wrong with this, but a father's words of encouragement ought to outnumber any constructive criticism four or five times to one. Look for qualities to affirm, lavish your daughter with praise when she does well, and be generous in your assessment of her.

God is generous with us and He expects us to be generous as well.

PRAY

God, thank You for Your many blessings, and please forgive me for those times when I have not been grateful or have been reluctant to share Your blessings with others. Help me to be a more generous man and to teach my daughter the virtue of generosity. Amen.

FLEX YOUR DAD MUSCLES

Have your daughter help you with a garage sale.

- You'll get time with your daughter.
- You'll get rid of a lot of clutter in your attic, closets, garage, and basement.
- You'll get some money that you can then turn around and give to some charity, ministry, or person in need.
- You'll have stuff left over that you can take to Goodwill or the Salvation Army.
- You'll receive the joy of having practiced generosity.

GENTLENESS

A gentle answer deflects anger,
but harsh words make tempers flare.
—Proverbs 15:1, NLT

R achel was a preacher's kid. Like many children of clergy, she knew a lot about God and the Bible. Sadly, she also knew a lot—too much, in fact—about the dark side of the "church world." She knew what it was like to live in a bubble and be scrutinized and criticized. She saw plenty of hypocrisy in the lives of church leaders and members. She was ridiculed at school. She, perhaps not surprisingly, developed questions and doubts, but felt there was no one she could confide in.

As a teenager, Rachel wanted one thing: to be out of the spiritual spotlight. She gravitated toward theater. There, in her high school drama department, she met free spirits. Slowly, she began pulling away from her parents and questioning their beliefs. Her dad's response was to insist she come to church even more. She complied outwardly but seethed inwardly. She soon became surly and bitter. Life in the Grace Church parsonage became one continual argument.

Graduating from high school and arriving on her university campus, Rachel finally felt free. She reinvented herself. She partied constantly, went to class sparingly (and usually drunk), met a Marine, and ended up in an emotionally abusive relationship.

Rachel continued down this dark, dangerous road for five-plus years. Internally she was miserable. She knew something desperately needed to change, but she didn't know what to do, and she was far too stubborn to ask for help. So what finally changed her?

Listen to her words:

"It wasn't my father. All he knew to do was to quote Bible verses at me. The minute he'd start in, I'd fire back at him, and the battle was on again.

"It was my Uncle Bob, of all people, who got through to me. He was actually a pastor too. He and my aunt were visiting. And, of course, he knew all about my miserable life, how screwed up I was. I remember we were sitting on the couch, and he asked me a few questions. I was bracing for another sermon, but it never came. Instead, he listened quietly. He didn't say a lot. In fact, I don't remember a single word he said. I just remember he was warm and disarming. I knew he didn't approve of my lifestyle, but still he was just...gentle. When I walked away from that conversation, something had shifted inside me. I remember, as I walked out the door, thinking, 'I'm done. I don't want to live like this anymore.'"

Uncle Bob is living proof of the truth of Proverbs 25:15: "Through patience a ruler can be persuaded, and a gentle tongue can break a bone" (NIV).

In Scripture, the word *gentleness* (sometimes translated as "meekness" as in the hymn about "Gentle Jesus, meek and mild") implies a strength that is kept under firm control. Biblical *gentleness* conveys the idea of courtesy, respect, the sort of men who used to be described as "the strong, silent type," a man who is secure in his strength and so refrains from unnecessary harshness, who believes his strength should be put at the service of others.

The Old Testament prophet Isaiah emphasized the uncommon gentleness of Israel's coming Messiah: "A bruised reed he will not break, and a smoldering wick he will not snuff out" (Isaiah 42:3, NIV).

It's no wonder, then, that when Christ came, He said, "Come to me, all of you who are weary and carry heavy burdens, and I will give you rest. Take my yoke upon you. Let me teach you, because *I am humble and gentle at heart*, and you will find rest for your souls. For my yoke is easy to bear, and the burden I give you is light" (Matthew 11:28–30, NLT, emphasis added).

Christ's encounter with the woman caught in adultery in John 8 is a striking example of His gentleness. When all the other religious leaders were ready to stone this guilty woman, Jesus came to her rescue, offering the perfect combination of grace and truth.

Here's what I know: dads of daughters need gentleness in spades. Girls can be maddening, defiant, and sassy. When they're not getting their way, daughters know how to punch all a father's buttons. I've seen some of the tiniest girls pitch the biggest fits. I've met many young women who can argue circles around their dads.

Smart dads could take a page from Rachel's Uncle Bob. Being soft-spoken and responding in a calm and rational manner is the best way to defuse tense situations. Let's say your daughter is worked up or "loaded for bear," as the old expression goes. She is geared up for a fight. If you assume a conciliatory tone and manner, it's like throwing her a curveball. It's like the angry dog that is barking and snarling as it chases a car—only to have the car suddenly stop. The poor dog is thrown for a loop. Now what?

You need to enter the conversation having first girded yourself with silent prayer—asking God to grant you self-control, kindness, and patience—and forethought. That's how the wise man responds.

Here are some areas where gentleness is especially needed:

- *In correcting your daughter.* "Brothers and sisters, if someone is caught in a sin, you who live by the Spirit should restore that person gently" (Galatians 6:1, NIV).
- *In talking to your daughter about spiritual matters.* "And if someone asks about your hope as a believer, always be ready

to explain it. But do this in a gentle and respectful way"
(1 Peter 3:15–16, NLT).

- *In everything you do.* "Always be humble and gentle" (Ephesians 4:2, NLT).

What Uncle Bob was to Rachel, you should be to your daughter—a quiet rock of strength, a kind and wise example. Ask God to help you develop the rare and precious quality of gentleness.

PRAY

God, I know when faced with tense situations I have a tendency to explode in anger, which is not strength but weakness, an inability to control my own emotions. Help me, Lord, instead to power up with humility, gentleness, and a quiet, soft-spoken strength. I pray that with the help of Your grace, my daughter might have a gentler, stronger, wiser father. Amen.

FLEX YOUR DAD MUSCLES

If you've been harsh with your daughter, confess that failure to God, accept His gentle forgiveness, and then go to your daughter and ask for her forgiveness too. Tell her you want to be a kinder and gentler father.

Then if you're really brave, ask her to fill out this "Gentleness Assessment":

When I do something my father doesn't like, he reacts in the following ways (*circle all that apply*):

He raises his voice.	He turns red.	He gets quiet.
He gets an angry look.	He yells at me.	He starts lecturing me.
He won't listen to what I say.	He throws or slams things.	He uses bad language.
He lets me know he loves me.	He asks me questions.	He starts arguing.
He makes faces at me.	He gets sarcastic.	He talks about consequences.
He makes threats.	He makes me feel stupid.	He mumbles under his breath.
He calls me names.	He measures his words.	He talks to me calmly.
He is warm and disarming.	He talks very slowly.	He looks disgusted with me.

Ask your daughter this question: *How do you wish I would respond to you in conflict situations?*

Week 20

GRIT

Blessed is the one who perseveres under trial because,
having stood the test, that person will receive the crown of life
that the Lord has promised to those who love him.
—James 1:12, NIV

G*rit*, determination and tenacity, is an indispensable quality of strong dads. It's the resolve, the strength of character, that says, "I'm not quitting. I will endure. I will persevere and reach the goal no matter what comes."

Whatever you choose to call it—grit, steel, backbone, mettle, perseverance, or endurance—your daughter needs you to display it.

Far too many times, fathers come up with all these great ideas for how they will raise their kids: great principles they want to pass on; healthy boundaries they intend to put in place; family traditions they want to instill. But having a wise plan is only half the battle—actually only about 15 percent of the battle. The real test comes in the day-to-day implementation of the plan. Action doesn't take genius; it requires grit.

Grit is about keeping your daughter on track. Why is it that fathers can relentlessly follow a plan at work or in training for a race, yet completely wilt when it comes to standing firm on the home front? I'll tell you why: pooped-out dads come home to daughters who are defiant, devious, and determined to get their way. Talk about gritty determination. I've seen tiny eight-year-olds who can wheedle and whine, moan and complain, press and beg, until they wear their fathers down and out. Suddenly dad is saying, "Whatever"—the very phrase he can't stand to hear coming out of his daughter's mouth.

While this is completely understandable, it's not acceptable. Men cannot continue to give all their best energy and focus to their work, then come home and give their families the leftovers and dregs. As I said in *Strong Fathers, Strong Daughters*, "If fathers recruited even 20 percent of the intellectual, physical, mental, and even emotional energy they spend at work and applied it to their relationships at home, we would live in an entirely different country" (p. 136). Dad, your grit is needed at home. It's when your daughter is pushing back the hardest that she most needs your perseverance.

I don't want to be an alarmist, but it only takes one moment of passivity for your daughter to end up in trouble. If you have clear and firm rules about whom your daughter can spend time with, and you enforce them 99 straight times but relent on the 100th time, you are playing with fire. You simply can't afford to go soft, not even for a moment. You can't afford to lower your guard or relax your standards. Grit means perpetual tenacity, not occasional backbone. Grit refuses to take a day off.

You might think (as dads often do) that loosening up and giving in will strengthen your bond with your daughter. If only you could be privy to the private thoughts and conversations of girls. You'll have to trust me on this. The truth is the exact opposite. Your daughter will respect you more if you *don't* relent. The moment you lose the grit of your convictions, you will lose stature in your daughter's eyes.

My personal and professional experience with daughters of all ages has unveiled for me this little-known secret: though girls talk in pained and annoyed tones about how strict their dads are, in their hearts they feel good about this fact. (The girls with permissive dads listen and feel envious.) Why is this so? Because when a dad stands his ground on the rules and boundaries set for his daughter, it communicates love and concern.

If you only had to stand up to your daughter a few times, the process wouldn't be so arduous and exhausting. But you will have to fight for her hundreds of times. You only have eighteen short years before she will be on her own. So you have to engage—and stay engaged. Every day you have to show up again. You can't go off duty. You always have to be gentle, but you can never go soft.

I warn you. She'll try every trick in the book: crying, begging, nagging, sulking, manipulating, dividing and conquering (trying to get her mother on her side), being sneaky, saying she hates you, lashing out, calling you names.

You have to be unflappable. You have to show true grit. You can see things she can't. You know what goes through a sixteen-year-old boy's mind when he sees a cute girl in a bikini. You know how even one drink can impair a seventeen-year-old's ability to drive. God has put you in your daughter's life to guide her, and good guides stay alert. They keep pointing and moving in the right direction, even when the way is tough.

Your daughter needs you to demonstrate grit in your dealings with her and in every other aspect of your life. When you persevere at a tough job, in a difficult marriage, in your faith, in friendships, in caring for aging parents—especially when those actions are costly—your daughter learns to persevere, to have grit, in her own life. The example you set for your precious little girl is priceless.

The Bible verse at the outset of this chapter speaks of the blessing and eventual reward of perseverance. And when it comes to fatherhood, dads either have grit or they quit. Don't be a quitter.

PRAY

God, help me to man up and remain strong, to demonstrate perseverance and grit, even when I'm tired, even in the face of repeated opposition. Give me the will to fight the good fight on behalf of my daughter. Amen.

FLEX YOUR DAD MUSCLES

Figure out an age-appropriate challenge to undertake with your daughter where you can both develop and demonstrate grit and determination—like training for and competing in a 5K race or starting a small business, or learning a new musical instrument or language.

Whatever path you choose, it will provide great opportunities to spend time with your daughter, work together, and see what makes her tick. It will be a bonding experience to last a lifetime. Make time for this; then go for it.

HONESTY

These are the things you are to do: Speak the truth to each
other, and render true and sound judgment in your courts.
—Zechariah 8:16, NIV

In part two of this book, "The Priorities of Strong Fathers," I wrote about
how strong fathers make integrity a top priority. Integrity, you'll recall,
suggests wholeness and completeness. A man with integrity doesn't live
a fragmented life—upstanding at church and conniving at the office. He is
high character *all the time*. He doesn't have a public persona and a different,
behind-the-scenes persona. What you see is truly who he is.

You can see, then, why honesty sits at the very heart of integrity. The
man who is committed to a life of integrity must possess the virtue of
honesty.

But what happens when daughters watch their dads shade or stretch
the truth or get caught in an outright lie?

Policeman: "Sir, have you been drinking?"

Dad: "Just one beer, Officer."

(His daughter knows for a fact it was *at least* three.)

Daughter: "Dad, if that show is so bad, how come you still watch it?"

Dad: "I only watched it for a few minutes; then I quit."

(He actually watched a few *episodes* and then started recording it on the DVR to watch at some point in the future.)

Daughter: "Dad, you promised you'd take me to get some ice cream."

Dad (eyes glued to the TV): "No, I said if you finished your homework by 7:00, we *might* have time to get some ice cream."

Daughter: "Well, I'm done with my homework, and it's 6:59."

Dad (glancing at his wrist): "My watch says 7:02. Plus the game's about to start. Sorry. Maybe tomorrow night?"

It's not just fathers who are guilty. We mothers are too. And it's a problem.

Studies indicate that deceit and deception have risen dramatically among kids over the last few decades. One survey determined that *three out of four* public high school students cheat on exams.

Your daughter is surrounded by friends for whom deception is natural. She lives in a dishonest culture whose lies can have a tragic impact on her.

She needs a better example—and your home needs to provide it.

I'm a big believer in authenticity and transparency. I'm convinced all secrets hurt. This is why I encourage husbands and wives to have a "No Secrets" policy.

And when your daughter sees you and your spouse living honestly, the results are amazing. When you don't hide behaviors, when you refuse to deny real faults or cover up flaws, your daughter will be more inclined to come clean about her own struggles.

I've seen it time and again in my medical practice: the girls who grow up in homes where the parents are primarily concerned about projecting a good image learn to keep the truth about who they are hidden from others. Girls with fathers who keep secrets are more inclined to marry men who will hide things. Don't be one of those fathers.

If you have secrets, come clean. Lead by example. It will be the beginning of a better, more joyful life.

Consider three biblical admonitions:

1. "Truthful words stand the test of time, but lies are soon exposed" (Proverbs 12:19, NLT).
2. "Rather, speaking the truth in love, we are to grow up in every way into him who is the head, into Christ" (Ephesians 4:15, ESV).
3. "Therefore each of you must put off falsehood and speak truthfully to your neighbor, for we are all members of one body" (Ephesians 4:25, NIV).

Talk over these passages with your daughter. Emphasize the importance of always being truthful. Stress that if you live a truthful life, you don't have to worry about one day being exposed. Be a truth teller—even when the truth is hard or humbling:

- Be honest with your finances (especially when doing taxes or filling out financial aid forms for your daughter's schooling).
- Be honest about that car you're selling (let your daughter hear you admit to the prospective buyer that the AC isn't exactly blowing cold air).
- Be honest in the way you describe events and situations (be careful not to fall into the habit of embellishing or exaggerating).
- Be honest in conflict situations. Without being combative, say the hard things that you need to say. Don't back down or chicken out.
- Be honest about your own failures. Some fathers, fearful of freaking out their daughters, hide dark secrets from their pasts (like a failed marriage, an arrest during college, or participation in an abortion). Your older daughter *can* handle these hard truths—and learn and grow from them. Don't let her

discover these things accidentally. You be the one to tell her. The act of sharing them will be an unforgettable life lesson in honesty.

One last thing: you'll need to teach your daughter to expect (even to demand) that friends and boyfriends be 100 percent truthful with her. After all, how can anyone have a satisfying and meaningful relationship that is founded on dishonesty?

Smart dads and strong dads are honest dads. William Shakespeare said it well: "No legacy is so rich as honesty."

PRAY

God, thank You for this challenge to be truthful. In our image-conscious, half-truth, tabloid culture, it is so easy to be "sort of" truthful or "almost" truthful or "mostly" truthful. But the old saying is true: a half truth is a whole lie. Show me the areas of my life where I struggle the most with honesty, and give me the courage to live with authenticity and integrity. Amen.

FLEX YOUR DAD MUSCLES

Sit down with your daughter and read and discuss Daniel 6 with her. This is the famous story of Daniel being thrown into the lions' den. It's a fantastic story about the importance of integrity and how, even in the face of grave danger, Daniel refused to live a lie or pretend to be something he wasn't. He was honest and authentic. And that authenticity brought him trouble and blessing.

You can talk about real-life pressures to deny the truth, to deny one's faith, to violate one's convictions, and how faith in God can give us courage. Here are some questions you might want to bat around with your daughter:

- What if Daniel had stopped praying? What would he have gained? What would he have lost?
- When are we tempted to hide who we really are?
- If people dug through our lives looking for "dirt," what would they find?

HUMILITY

And all of you, dress yourselves in humility
as you relate to one another, for "God opposes the
proud but gives grace to the humble."
—1 Peter 5:5, NLT

Whenever I talk about the importance of humility (which is frequently), I typically get a lot of raised eyebrows. Here's why I'm convinced the best fathers are humble fathers:

What humility is and isn't. Contrary to popular belief, "being humble" doesn't mean being a doormat for others. *Humility* isn't a synonym for *weakness* or *self-loathing*.

Maybe the best way to think about it is to think of those football players who are stars on the field, but who are gentlemanly off of it; who don't boast or brag; who talk about the team rather than themselves; who don't let stardom go to their heads.

Humility is about having a right and healthy perspective of basic human worth—your own worth as well as others' worth. Humility is rooted in the belief that dignity and significance are God-given. Though each person is different, no one has more intrinsic value than another. Everyone matters. Everyone is important. Only this mindset is able to ground us, guarding us from the extremes of either self-exaltation or self-deprecation.

In his classic book *Mere Christianity*, C. S. Lewis noted that pride—the opposite of humility—fights bitterly against this idea of people having equal value. "Pride is essentially competitive," Lewis wrote. A proud man "gets no pleasure out of having something, only out of having more of it than the next man." Thus the proud man is utterly self-centered and obsessed with vaunting himself above others. He is forever comparing, always measuring himself against others. As a result, his pride is constantly swelling ("Ha, I am better") or deflating ("Woe, I am inferior"). Either way, all the proud man is left with is scorn—either for others or for himself.

The humble man, by contrast, doesn't spend time ranking people or agonizing about where he fits in the cultural pecking order. Lewis put it succinctly: "True humility is not thinking less of yourself; it is thinking of yourself less." In truth, humility is looking beyond yourself with a desire to serve others.

How we cultivate humility. The Christian faith is rooted in two great truths that, properly understood, lead to healthy humility. The first truth is that we are not "okay." In fact, we are sinful and spiritually destitute. We desperately need God's forgiveness, mercy, and help. Embracing this idea keeps us from becoming big-headed, or arrogant.

The second great truth is that God loves us fully and completely *as we are*. Embracing this idea keeps us from succumbing to despair and fills us with gratitude, hope, and confidence. After all, if God Almighty accepts us in Christ, and if He is for us, who can be against us?

Taken together, these two truths are incredibly good news: despite my mess, I matter infinitely to God. So does everyone else.

Why humility is necessary. Cultivating humility is critical for at least two reasons:

One, *pride is deadly*. Proverbs 16:18 warns, "Pride goes before destruc-
tion, and haughtiness before a fall" (NLT). C. S. Lewis called pride "the
great sin" and pointed out that it was through pride that the devil became
the devil. Pride is at the root of most of the heartache in the world. It's
surely behind every conflict. Pride is an enemy of marriage and the killer
of many friendships.

Two, *humility is liberating*. It frees us from grandiose, even delusional,
opinions of self. Humility frees us from the discouraging and destructive
habit of comparing ourselves to others. It frees us from the paralyzing fear
of what others *might* think about us. It also frees us from self-absorption,
enabling us to move toward others and serve them.

As we allow humility to reign in our hearts, we begin to hear different
and better voices than what we hear from the world:

- Humility assures, "Your worth is not in what you do, what
  you have, or how others view you, but in the fact that you are
  made in the image of God."
- Humility asks, "What do you have that God hasn't given
  you?" (1 Corinthians 4:7, NLT), thereby reminding us that our
  abilities and wealth, even our very lives, are a gift from God.
- Humility reminds, "Your failures don't alter the fact that you
  are loved and valuable."
- Humility says, "Others are not your competitors or enemies;
  they are fellow creatures you can serve and from whom you
  can learn."
- Humility challenges, "Instead of concentrating on what you
  want, give yourself to what others need."
- Humility whispers, "The world doesn't revolve around you—
  therefore you don't have to be the center of attention or the
  focus of every conversation."

In the verse at the beginning of this chapter we read that God opposes the proud but gives grace to the humble. Which sounds like the better deal to you: being opposed by God or receiving grace from God?

Passing on humility. It's not enough for fathers to cultivate humility in their own lives. You also need to make a concerted and intentional effort to teach your children this rare virtue.

I said earlier that it is important to praise your daughter—and it is. But that praise should be based in reality, in honesty and sincerity. No good is achieved by gushing effusively about everything your daughter does, or telling her that she is—or needs to be—the prettiest, smartest, most popular girl you know.

Deep inside, your daughter knows she's good at some things and not so good at other things. She often views her talents more realistically than you do. The harder you push the praise button when it's undeserved, the more she questions herself: *Is this the reason Dad loves me so much?*

You want your daughter to be confident, yet humble. So give her honest praise and teach her that whatever her strengths or weaknesses, we are all equal in the eyes of God. It's really not that hard a lesson to learn. However much the media promote the idea of self, flattering the self, and measuring people's worth in terms of money or celebrity, and so on, bragging, self-centeredness, and egotism are not usually attractive qualities when we see them in other people. We just need to guard against those temptations within ourselves.

The single best way to teach humility is to live it yourself. If you talk about humility but your daughter routinely hears you name-dropping, measuring yourself against friends or neighbors, putting others down, or gloating about successes, she will learn pride.

On the other hand, if she sees you being honest about your failures, quietly serving your family, sincerely apologizing when wrong, and treating all people with the same grace and kindness, she will learn humility. When you show through your acts of service and gracious words that nothing (and no one) is beneath you, you have an enormous impact on your daughter.

My challenge to you: live your life in such a way that when your daughter hears the word *humility*, she thinks of you.

PRAY

God, forgive my sins of pride, for putting myself first, for not setting a better example of humility for my daughter. Help me to remember that we are all equal in your eyes, even as we are different, and that I should always seek to exalt You and not myself. Amen.

FLEX YOUR DAD MUSCLES

Ask yourself these four hard questions:

- Am I frequently critical of friends, family members, or coworkers?
- Do I immediately judge people—deciding whether they are worth my time?
- Am I condescending when I address service staff, junior employees, my wife, my children?
- Am I open to constructive criticism?

If you answered yes to any of these questions, make a list of ways you could do better, and act on that list.

One constructive step that every father can take is charitable work—there is no quicker path to humility, and joy, than serving others. Find a community or church project where you can help out. Bring your daughter with you, and let her see you work for others with a humble and happy heart.

JOY

A cheerful heart is good medicine,
but a crushed spirit dries up the bones.
—Proverbs 17:22, NIV

At a track meet for my daughter, I glanced down the hill at the four-lane highway below. About a half mile away, I noticed a large, gray-haired cyclist making his way toward us. After a few moments, I realized it was Peter, a man whose daughter, Elizabeth, also ran track.

Peter and Elizabeth were bonded by their love of athletics and the great outdoors. When she was little, he would often take her on walks in the woods. In the fourth grade when she took up running, he would often jog with her after work at the high school track.

On this occasion Peter was still dressed in his work clothes. With his sleeves rolled up, his dress slacks tucked into his socks, and his tie flapping in the breeze, he was a comical sight. Sweating profusely, Peter chugged up the hill and parked his bike. Then without even bothering to fix his hair or remove his trousers from his socks, he made his way over to where his daughter was sitting. Spotting her dad, Elizabeth sprang to her feet and began to run toward him. Peter smiled and broke into a jog. Lowering his six-foot-four-inch frame, he grabbed his daughter by the waist and tossed her high into the air. She squealed with delight and flailed like a rag doll. Catching her, he swung her around and gave her a big hug. Giggling, she scooted off to run in her event.

It was such a heartwarming interaction between a father and a daughter. And maybe the primary thing it conveyed was *joy*—the joy in a dad's heart for the daughter he loves.

Joy is one of the cardinal virtues of great fathers. It's an oft-mentioned subject in the Bible. In fact, the word is found almost 250 times in the New International Version of the Bible.

The biblical word refers to a deep and abiding gladness. We might feel upbeat when someone compliments us or when we hit every green light on the way to work, but joy isn't a temporary emotion, it is a state of mind.

The clear testimony of the biblical writers is that joy is experienced by those who cultivate a conscious and deep awareness of spiritual reality. In other words, joy is inextricably tied to God. This is why the apostle Paul stated, "But the fruit of the Spirit is...joy" (Galatians 5:22, NIV).

Trusting in the biblical claim that God is with us brings joy. This is what prompted David to exclaim, "You make known to me the path of life; *you will fill me with joy in your presence*, with eternal pleasures at your right hand" (Psalms 16:11, NIV, emphasis added).

When we are able to *trust* that God is in control of not only the world but our very lives, *believe* that He is for us, and *rest* in the promise that He is in the process of restoring the world and "making all things new" (Revelation 21:5), all these things combine to stimulate a joyful mindset in us. This explains why people of faith down through the ages have been able to face terrible trials with confidence and peace. They understand that behind this real world with its real problems and pains there is a deeper reality still. It's because our happiness hinges not on circumstances but on the blessings that are ours in Christ that Paul exhorted the believers in

Thessalonica: "Rejoice always" (1 Thessalonians 5:16, NASB). Joy is dependent not on temporary feelings but on eternal facts.

So how does a father cultivate this priceless trait in his heart and create a joyful culture in his home?

Trust God. During His earthly ministry, Christ once pulled a small child over to Himself and said to the watching crowd, "Truly I tell you, unless you change and become like little children, you will never enter the kingdom of heaven" (Matthew 18:3, NIV).

What is it about children that Jesus was saying we should emulate? Kids (at least up until a certain age) are unpretentious and trusting. Think of your own daughter. When she was four or five she trusted you implicitly to take care of everything. If you said, "Let's go on a trip," she gladly piled in the car. She didn't stress over what you were going to eat, where you were going to sleep, or how you were going to pay the credit card bill when you got home. (Most of that never even occurred to her.) In her trusting soul, she was free to sit back and enjoy herself, to "ooh" and "ah" over the sights.

Joy is like that. It stems from a deep sense that "Someone has me." A dad can be joyful like that when he embraces the idea that God is watching over his life, his family, his employment situation, his financial status. Joy says, "I don't have to be stern and grim because I am loved and kept."

Be positive. In one of his letters, the apostle Paul penned these words (that are worth pondering, if not memorizing): "Fix your thoughts on what is true, and honorable, and right, and pure, and lovely, and admirable. Think about things that are excellent and worthy of praise" (Philippians 4:8, NLT).

In other words, be positive. Most of the stories we hear are negative and depressing. Better to fill your mind with uplifting thoughts. If checking the news headlines always leaves you discouraged and anxious, consider taking a break from that. Focus on upbeat stories. Instead of dwelling on gloomy subjects, accentuate the good things in life—the day's highlights, inspiring stories from the lives of friends and from the world of athletics. Let your home be an oasis from all the negativity in our culture. Also forbid abusive speech, name-calling, and ugly talk (and don't fall into this yourself). True joy is rooted in the confidence that God's plans for us are plans for good.

Celebrate often. Don't wait for birthdays or anniversaries to celebrate. Make a big fuss over smaller achievements. If your daughter is cavity-free, or she received an A+ on a spelling quiz, or your wife started a blog, or the dog learned to roll over, party! Parade around the house. Clap. Cheer. Turn up the music and dance. In other words, be silly. Laugh. Let your whimsical side come out and play.

Bob Goff, the exuberant and adventurous author of *Love Does*, wrote, "I think a father's job, when it's done best, is to get down on both knees, lean over his children's lives, and whisper, 'Where do you want to go?' Every day God invites us on the same kind of adventure. It's not a trip where He sends us a rigid itinerary, He simply invites us. God asks what it is He's made us to love, what it is that captures our attention, what feeds that deep indescribable need of our souls to experience the richness of the world He made. And then, leaning over us, He whispers, 'Let's go do *that* together.'"

Dads need to be joyful because the world is a grim place. Dads also need to lighten up because, as C. S. Lewis so wisely observed, "joy is the serious business of heaven."

Will you give your daughter lots of memories of her daddy laughing and being joyful?

PRAY

God, forgive me for being too somber and serious so much of the time. Help me lighten up. I want to be marked by joy. Amen.

Flex Your Dad Muscles

Do something completely silly and unpredictable this week. Here are some ideas to spark your thinking and make some joyful memories:

- Dress up in goofy costumes and take pictures (to attach to the fridge or post on Facebook).
- Invent a new game and play it together.
- Eat dessert first.
- Go outside and play in the rain (or in the sprinkler).
- Let your daughter put makeup all over you and fix your hair.
- Act out scenes from your favorite movie and videotape yourselves.
- Invent a new recipe together.
- Declare "prank week" at your house and see who can trick another family member the best (this will require laying down a few rules).

Week 24

PATIENCE

Love is patient, love is kind.
—1 Corinthians 13:4, NASB

When Jackie came home for Christmas during her second year at Vanderbilt, her father, Tom, was stunned. His daughter looked terrible. She was emaciated. Her eyes were dark. She claimed to have no appetite. Something was clearly wrong.

Tom wondered if she was suffering from academic stress, or maybe the aftereffects of his divorce. Or perhaps her obvious trouble was due to the fact that he had been something of a workaholic in his job as an accountant when Jackie and her brothers were younger. *Maybe she has cancer...or AIDS*, he thought. Yet she was well enough to exercise frantically and furiously for ninety minutes at a time.

Tom called everyone he could think of—colleagues, friends, even his ex-wife. Nobody seemed to know what to do. Finally one day during the holiday break he blurted out to his daughter, "Why don't you ever eat?"

She exploded in fury at her befuddled dad. Not knowing where to turn, Tom called a physician friend. She told Tom, "It sounds to me like your daughter may have an eating disorder."

The friend was right. Jackie was diagnosed with anorexia nervosa. She ended up needing many months of extensive medical treatment. Even after that she battled a lot of destructive thought patterns. During an office visit, I got to watch Tom patiently speak truth into the life of his daughter. That is, I found out what he had been doing day after day and month after month. With gentleness and determination, Tom was helping Jackie fight the demons in her head.

She was eventually able to return to Vanderbilt. While Tom would never claim credit for healing Jackie's anorexia, I'm sure she would say his patient involvement was a key ingredient in her recovery.

It is easy for an impatient father to blow his stack. It takes great strength to ignore your frustration and be patient. That self-control, self-mastery, will save *you* from embarrassment and remorse, and your calm, firm, reasonable voice and example will greatly benefit your daughter.

Here are some great biblical passages on patience. I promise you, they're worth pondering:

- "Finishing is better than starting. Patience is better than pride" (Ecclesiastes 7:8, NLT).
- "Therefore, as God's chosen people, holy and dearly loved, clothe yourselves with compassion, kindness, humility, gentleness and patience" (Colossians 3:12, NIV).
- "Whoever is patient has great understanding, but one who is quick-tempered displays folly" (Proverbs 14:29, NIV).
- "Always be humble and gentle. Be patient with each other, making allowance for each other's faults because of your love" (Ephesians 4:2, NLT).

I want to be clear. Patience is not passivity. It's not being oblivious to misbehavior or looking the other way.

What it does mean is having the inner strength and self-control not to be provoked.

Who do you most respect (and who do you think your daughter will most respect)—a man who is cool, calm, or collected, or a raving hothead?

A patient man doesn't rant at traffic jams or fly off the handle when he trips over his daughter's skates for the third day in a row or slam his hand on the table in anger if he drops his buttered toast on the floor. He accepts these things for what they are—minor inconveniences that aren't made any better by losing his cool.

The best example of patience is, of course, God Himself. The Bible is full of passages in which God demonstrates His infinitely patient nature. Let me give you just one. In the book of Nehemiah, when the ancient Israelites declared a day of fasting and mourning to confess their national sins and seek God's forgiveness and favor, they recounted their not-so-stellar spiritual track record as a people:

> But our ancestors were proud and stubborn, and they paid no attention to your commands. They refused to obey and did not remember the miracles you had done for them. Instead, they became stubborn and appointed a leader to take them back to their slavery in Egypt. But you are a God of forgiveness, gracious and merciful, *slow to become angry*, and rich in unfailing love. You did not abandon them, even when they made an idol shaped like a calf and said, "This is your god who brought you out of Egypt!" They committed terrible blasphemies. (Nehemiah 9:16–18, NLT, emphasis added)

The point is this: If God can be so patient with His children in the face of ultimate rebellion, how can we do less with our children when they merely act like immature kids?

We could trot out every cliché here to remind ourselves why parents need to cultivate patience: "Good things come to those who wait." "Rome wasn't built in a day." "Slow and steady wins the race." "Life is a marathon not a sprint." "You're not growing squash or bamboo, you're growing oak trees."

The point is, your daughter is growing up, it's a process, so cut her some slack. Keep teaching, loving, correcting, and reminding. In time, it will come together. You will see positive changes. Your patience will pay off handsomely.

In the meantime, when she's defiant and violates rules that you and your wife have set forth, discipline is appropriate and necessary. But make sure you administer consequences patiently, not in a spirit of frustration, irritation, or anger.

When she can't seem to get the hang of something—math homework or remembering to signal before she gets in the left-hand turning lane—be careful. Watch your attitude, your facial expressions, and your tone of voice. Her failure to "get it" is not because she's not trying—daughters want desperately to please their fathers. Her inability is because something isn't yet clicking for her. Don't make her feel stupid. Take a deep breath and come at it again. Be patient. If you do, she'll respect you all the more. As Solomon said, "Fools vent their anger, but the wise quietly hold it back" (Proverbs 29:11, NLT).

PRAY

God, help me cultivate the virtue of patience, of self-control, of quiet strength, so that I might be a better witness to your own enduring patience and love and so that I might be a better father to my daughter and husband to my wife. Amen.

FLEX YOUR DAD MUSCLES

Do a *patience inventory* in your own life. Think about the following questions (be honest when you answer):

- Are you patient in heavy traffic? When you have to wait in long lines?
- Do you get ticked when machines and gadgets won't work properly for you?
- Do you get weary and snappy when your young daughter asks you a million "why" questions about everything under the sun?
- Do you get visibly frustrated when you have to remind your daughter about certain things multiple times a day?
- Do you catch yourself saying (or yelling) these kinds of things to your daughter: *When are you ever going to start being responsible? How many times do I have to tell you? We just talked about this! I'm not going to tell you again!*

If you are feeling especially brave, gather up the courage to ask your wife and daughter, "On a scale of one to ten, with one being 'not at all' and ten being 'off the charts incredible,' how patient would you say I am?"

Week 25

PURITY

I made a covenant with my eyes not to
look lustfully at a young woman.
—Job 31:1, NIV

I f there is a bigger temptation or greater snare to men than pornography,
I don't know what it is.

I have a husband and son, and I know the temptations they face.
They, and you, are battered constantly with sexual imagery. In 2006 I
wrote, "Sexualized advertising has done tremendous harm to young
girls and women. But that harm multiplies threefold for men" (*Strong
Fathers, Strong Daughters*, p. 154). Today, I'm inclined to say the harm
is tenfold.

The seduction is relentless, and with our ubiquitous laptops, tablets,
and smartphones, it's always just a few clicks or swipes away. It feels very
innocuous. *No one will be hurt*, a little voice whispers. But the statistics
and personal stories combine to shout out a vastly different truth: pornography hurts *everyone*.

The link between pornography and sexual violence against women
and children is clear.

And the fact that pornography is devastating to men is undeniable.

There is no manliness in pornography, there is only shame, yet many men become addicted to the thing that shames them.

Make no mistake. Porn is evil. It wrecks lives.

Thanks to the Internet, porn feels very private and secretive. *No one will ever know*, the voice whispers seductively. But recent hacking scandals demonstrate that nothing done online is truly anonymous. All your searching and clicking is being monitored. How else do you think those ads for electric drills began showing up in your browser right when you were in the market for an electric drill? What happens in secret eventually gets shouted from the rooftops. Jesus Himself said, "For there is nothing hidden that will not be disclosed, and nothing concealed that will not be known or brought out into the open" (Luke 8:17, NIV).

King Solomon, universally regarded as the wisest man to ever live, was so concerned about the dangers of sexual immorality he spent the better part of three chapters of the famous book of Proverbs graphically pleading with his sons to be pure. Nowhere in literature do we find a clearer picture of the anatomy of sexual temptation:

> So she seduced him with her pretty speech and enticed him with her flattery. He followed her at once, like an ox going to the slaughter. He was like a stag caught in a trap, awaiting the arrow that would pierce its heart. He was like a bird flying into a snare, little knowing it would cost him his life. So listen to me, my sons, and pay attention to my words. Don't let your hearts stray away toward her. Don't wander down her wayward path. For she has been the ruin of many; many men have been her victims. Her house is the road to the grave. Her bedroom is the den of death. (Proverbs 7:21–27, NLT)

Men (and their wives) who know firsthand the destructive nature of pornography realize just how true these words are.

Pornography is a form of prostitution. Would you consort with prostitutes?

And there is something else to remember: you are a father. You have a daughter. Every woman who is a prostitute or in a pornographic picture or video is someone else's daughter. She does not deserve to be victimized like that, and you, if anything, should be fighting against her victimization, not acting as a voyeuristic bystander.

Every man needs to put on the armor of purity, to make a conscious effort to pray every time every he is tempted, to remember always to put God first.

In Psalm 119, we find some great counsel about how men can fight for purity. The psalmist wrote:

> How can a young man keep his way pure?
> By keeping *it* according to Your word.
> With all my heart I have sought You;
> do not let me wander from Your commandments.
> Your word I have treasured in my heart,
> that I may not sin against You. (Psalms 119:9–11, NASB)

The psalmist suggests that the greatest need of a man's soul is God. That's why he says he seeks God with "all [his] heart." What's more, he expresses his intention to align his life and his desires to the truth of God's "word."

In a world full of lies, we need the truth of God's Word. When confronted with the enslaving lies of pornography, we need the liberating truth of God.

I have seen the destructive power of pornography. I have seen reputations ruined, daughters shattered, marriages wrecked, and families torn apart by pornography's glossy lies. Millions of men regret their choices to click and look. I don't know one good man who would say, "I'm so glad I made the choice to look at those pictures or videos." Nothing good ever comes from giving in to the temptation to view pornography.

The Apostle Paul tells us that "The temptations in your life are no different from what others experience. And God is faithful. He will not allow the temptation to be more than you can stand. When you are tempted, he will show you a way out so that you can endure" (1 Corinthians 10:13, NLT).

That "way out" is most likely prayer. It is our way to talk to God and ask for His mercy and help. Make use of it when you are tempted to do wrong.

If you are pure of heart, be humbly thankful—and treat the Internet with a healthy fear.

If you are addicted to pornography make an immediate vow to stop. Confess your sins to God and ask for His forgiveness. And be a real man who controls his passions and who is honest and pure.

PRAY

God, please help me to avoid sexual temptation, and to love You more than I love anything else. I pray that with the help of Your grace I might live a life of honesty and purity. Amen.

FLEX YOUR DAD MUSCLES

Here are some practical ways to put on the armor of purity:

- Simple but effective: remember the admonition from the Lord's Prayer, "lead us not into temptation." Avoid temptations to sin by staying far away from movies, pictures, and links that might get you into trouble.
- Keep a Bible next to your computer mouse.
- Remember that you are never alone—God is always watching over you.

Week 26

SELF-CONTROL

*A man without self-control is like a city
broken into and left without walls.*
—Proverbs 25:28, ESV

In February 2015, the *New York Times Magazine* published a chilling article entitled "How One Stupid Tweet Blew Up Justine Sacco's Life." The hard-to-believe story details how a thirty-year-old corporate communications director thoughtlessly fired off a sarcastic tweet to her 170 Twitter followers as she boarded a flight to South Africa. By the time Miss Sacco had landed in Cape Town eleven hours later, her careless comment was trending worldwide and tens of thousands of angry tweets had been sent in response to her "joke." The young woman ended up losing her job. Socially she was ostracized. Emotionally she was humiliated.

Here's a sobering truth most people only learn the hard way: it is possible to do something in a moment that will give you heartache for a lifetime. Our careless actions can (and sometimes do) have long-term consequences. When we follow every fleeting impulse, we are defenseless and vulnerable—in the words of Solomon above, we are like "a city broken into and left without walls." Clearly, we must acquire the virtue of self-control.

Self-control is the ability to master one's desires and restrain one's impulses. The self-controlled man commands himself. He doesn't give in to whims. He isn't at the mercy of his urges and instincts. He thinks before he speaks. He weighs consequences before he acts. He makes choices on the basis of what is wisest and best for the long-term, not according to what seems expedient in the moment.

Self-control always leads to a better life—whether that self-control means restraining your temper so that you don't say something you might later regret, or answering that 5:00 a.m. alarm so you can get in a three-mile run before work, or setting aside time every day to read the Bible. Every successful man you have ever known has gotten where he is because of self-control.

Here's the thing about self-control. It's a virtue you can cultivate, but ultimately it's a gift from God, something He has implanted into our souls. The apostle Paul said: "But the fruit of the Spirit is...self-control" (Galatians 5:22–23, NIV).

We find the spirit of self-control when we allow the Spirit of God to control us. We might grow weary and discouraged on our own, but God is never weary or discouraged; if we rely on Him, He will give us the strength to control ourselves.

Self-controlled people are secure people. They know they won't be overthrown by their emotions, by temptations, by provocations.

As with every other virtue, your daughter needs to see the virtue of self-control in your own life. Let her see you put duty (like mowing the lawn), before pleasure (like watching the big game on TV). And teach her the same virtues of self-restraint and delayed gratification: like no TV before all her homework is done. Set the rules and expect her to be accountable for them.

Children gain confidence when they have rules to follow and standards to meet. The happiest children are those who practice self-control; the most miserable children are those who are *out of control.*

Teach self-control in word and deed. Emphasize it. Expect it. And your daughter will grow into the poised, responsible young woman you want her to be.

PRAY

Lord, help me to be man enough to control myself, to find that gift of the Spirit that is self-control. Amen.

FLEX YOUR DAD MUSCLES

Make a "vow night" where everyone gets together and vows to stop a bad habit or take on a good one.

Dad, you go first. Share the habit you want to break (like not getting upset in traffic) or, if you are *really* brave, ask your daughter or wife what habit *she* would like to see you break.

For your children, the vows can be as simple as making their beds every day or committing to flossing every night.

Close by saying that no matter what the challenge, each person *can* succeed, because "the fruit of the Spirit is...self-control."

THE HABITS OF STRONG FATHERS

Week 27

ACCEPTING

Therefore, accept one another, just as Christ
also accepted us to the glory of God.
—Romans 15:7, NASB

Why are relationships so hard? Why do kids bully other kids? Why do some married couples, once crazily in love, divorce? Why do so many of us tell innumerable "white lies"? Why do we often feel, like St. Paul, that "I do not understand what I do. For what I want to do I do not do, but what I hate I do" (Romans 7:15 NIV).

Theologians attribute this to "original sin" or "the fall of man," recorded in Genesis 3 of the Bible, when Adam and Eve disobeyed God by eating the forbidden fruit from the tree of the knowledge of good and evil.

We have inherited their original sin in our human nature, which means we often fall prey to temptation. Too often we put ourselves before others; we put our own desires ahead of God's law.

Sin makes relationships difficult. And if they are difficult for adults, who have lots of experience with human interaction, we should remember how difficult they can be for children or teenagers.

Your daughter learns about relationships, early on, directly from her relationship with you. This is when she learns to trust, to build an emotional bond, to not be afraid to engage with others. It's important that your daughter knows that you love her for who she is, without qualification. If she believes, or realizes, that your approval is based on other criteria—her looks, her grades, her athletic performance—it will build distance between you, because that's not the totality of your daughter. If she knows there are things about her that you don't like or won't accept, she'll try to hide them—in unhealthy ways. If she's upset because she's gained a little weight—and maybe been teased about it at school—and then hears you making snarky comments about overweight people, she's going to close off some of herself. If your daughter feels rejected, she won't openly share her thoughts and feelings because she won't fully trust you.

You see the same dynamic with children whose fathers are overly critical, or who yell a lot, or who are emotionally volatile (often because of alcoholism). Kids walk on eggshells. They can never let down their guard. If the slightest misstep might result in an epic rant (or worse), they're not likely to open up about their innermost thoughts or feelings.

Acceptance is about unconditional love. It flourishes when a father intentionally sets out to create a home environment where his children can feel safe. How do fathers do this? How can you create a safe home where emotional intimacy is the rule, not the rare exception?

First, find a place, like maybe the swing on the back porch, where your daughter can talk to you without other family members eavesdropping or interrupting.

Second, spend time with your daughter. Lots of it. She needs your presence in her life. Nothing communicates love and acceptance more than your choosing to spend time with her. I realize some jobs require long hours and create special challenges, but if at all possible, connect with her in the morning. Give her a smile and a big hug. Share a kind, encouraging word. If your work schedule permits, be the one who takes her to school. Then try to be home in time for supper.

When she's little, be the one to put her to bed. Create rituals for that time—reading (or singing) to her, saying prayers with her, and giving her butterfly kisses. And don't stop when she's older. Keep popping your head in her room and assuring her of your love.

No matter what her age, establish the habit of daddy-daughter dates—every week without fail. Take up a hobby together. Many fathers soon discover that their children are their favorite companions.

Third, as you create an atmosphere of trust, remember the Golden Rule. Jesus said, "Treat others the same way you want them to treat you" (Luke 6:31, NASB).

When you are troubled or sad, you probably don't want to be chided or lectured. So don't do that to your daughter. Don't interrupt her if she opens up to you. Just listen. Respect her. Pray for her.

In my book *Your Kids at Risk: How Teen Sex Threatens Our Sons and Daughters*, I told the story of a dad who rented a house in Europe for a month every year while his kids were teenagers. No friends. No television. No work. This was a concentrated time for the family to be together in a strange place (with none of the usual distractions from home).

Initially, the teens complained of boredom. They begged to go home. In fact, the whole family was edgy and irritable. But after a few days, the family began working together—making plans, compromising on activities, accepting each other's interests—and soon they were hiking and shopping and sightseeing and cooking and, yes, laughing together. They learned one another's likes and dislikes, interests and quirks, and loved each other's company all the more.

I realize few families can spend a month in Europe. But the same scenario can be played out at a summer cabin or even in your own home. The point is to create an environment where your daughter feels loved and accepted and safe. That starts wherever you are.

PRAY

God, I want my daughter to trust me. I want to be the kind of father who is warm and accepting, and who makes her feel safe. Please help me to be the good father who practices unconditional love and acceptance. Amen.

FLEX YOUR DAD MUSCLES

Take a day or a week and turn off all the distracting electronic devices in your house. You can keep the lights on, and the electronic stove and microwave are fine, but no smartphone, no checking e-mail or Facebook, no video games, no glazed watching of television.

The great missionary martyr Jim Elliot once said, "Wherever you are, be all there." That's great advice for dads. Leave work at work. When you're at home, put on your fathering hat. Give your daughter some serious face time. See if you can discover something about her today that you never knew before.

Ask her about her day. Engage. Make eye contact. Ask follow-up questions. Share her joys. Commiserate in her sorrows. Accept her as the immortal soul that she is.

ADORING

For the Lord your God is living among you.
He is a mighty savior. He will take delight in you with
gladness. With his love, he will calm all your fears.
He will rejoice over you with joyful songs.
—Zephaniah 3:17, NLT

In his acclaimed book *Wild at Heart,* author John Eldredge writes these arresting words: "The deep cry of a little girl's heart is *am I lovely?* Every woman needs to know that she is exquisite and exotic and *chosen.* This is core to her identity, the way she bears the image of God. *Will you pursue me? Do you delight in me? Will you fight for me?* ... A little girl looks to her father to know if she is lovely" (p. 182).

After decades of raising girls and working with girls, I can only say, "Yes. Amen. This is a profound truth." All the research conclusively shows that girls who grow up with attentive, loving fathers do better in every area of life.

This isn't pop psychology, by the way. This is the way God intended for things to be. Look again at the verse above. Notice how God Himself is described. He's not only strong ("a mighty savior), but He delights in His children. He wants to love the fear right out of us. With gladness (not a reluctant sense of duty), He rejoices and sings over us. In all this, the ultimate Father lays out a pattern for earthly dads to follow: Delight in your kids. Rejoice over them. Make sure your daughter knows she is both loved and lovely—that you are crazy about her.

Here's what your daughter is looking for—the two A words:

Attention. She feels most loved (and lovely) when you pay attention to her, when you notice the little details of her life; when you engage with her she feels cherished. When she goes on a date and comes home at midnight and finds you waiting up for her, she feels special. Sure, you can ask how her time was, but the mere fact that you cared enough to make sure she got home safely makes her feel deeply loved.

Adoration. Women want to feel that someone in their lives thinks the world of them. Adoration says, "I'm for you. I believe in you. I think you're amazing." Eldredge is right. Your daughter is looking to you to answer the question *am I lovely?* When you, as her father, affirm her, you boost her emotional confidence in a uniquely powerful way that makes her feel strong and complete. She will not feel the need to look for affirmation, because she's found it.

When you adore you daughter, and express that adoration openly, it gives her a necessary sense of security. If she doesn't get that security and affirmation from you, it can lead to dangerous situations later on, when she seeks it from places you might not want.

Our world degrades women, and the best protection you can give her against this is fatherly adoration. Don't stint on it.

Here are some practical ways to answer the nagging question—*am I lovely*—of her feminine soul:

Tell her you love her. You might come from an unexpressive home. You might feel uncomfortable with such "mushy" communication. Press through the discomfort. Every daughter needs—often—to see into her dad's adoring eyes and hear the words *I love you.* Tell her as often as you can.

Express adoration. Let her know that she is the joy and delight of your life. And don't be economical with your words. Girls love words, and they bond through words. So tell your daughter what you admire about her and tell her why. I promise that if you are sincere, your words will change who she is becoming.

Believe in her. Examine her character and find what is good and praiseworthy in her. Look deeply into her life and discover her natural abilities. Then, communicate to her that you are her "number one fan." Tell her a version of what Gandalf told Bilbo Baggins in *The Hobbit*: "There is more to you than you know." Assure her over and over that she is smarter than she thinks, wiser than she believes, and more capable than she realizes. Communicating this is extremely important because most girls, especially during adolescence, feel terribly inadequate, dumb, and unattractive. You need to really amp up your positive comments during the tough times and help her combat these feelings. Even if the two of you have a tendency to clash constantly, look for ways to show her that you believe in her.

Don't comment on her weight—EVER. Don't praise her for being thin and don't make teasing or chiding comments about her being chubby or needing to lose a few pounds. No matter what you say about her weight, you will sow seeds of insecurity. I can't tell you the number of messes I've seen that stemmed from fathers innocently (or insensitively) commenting about their daughters' weight.

Comment on her looks rarely. I know this feels counterintuitive. Shouldn't every girl know that her dad thinks she's beautiful? Of course; but don't overdo it. You don't want her to feel like physical appearance is a top priority to you. Remember, when you comment on something, it lets the hearer know that the topic is significant to you (otherwise why would you comment on it?). You want to be sure that your daughter knows that what you really cherish most about her is her inner beauty. So talk chiefly about that.

Every girl is asking the huge question: *Am I lovely?* Give your daughter the answer that will free her from fear and set her up for a lifetime of success. Be a dad who excels in adoring his daughter.

PRAY

God, I am struck by how much power I have as a dad to influence my daughter for good or for ill. Forgive me for the times I've been so preoccupied that I've missed opportunities to speak into my daughter's heart. Today, give me creativity and courage to move toward her so that I can love and cherish her in good and life-changing ways. Amen.

FLEX YOUR DAD MUSCLES

Do something tangible to demonstrate how special your daughter is to you.

Simple things can mean a lot. Little traditions don't have to take a lot of time. If you get up earlier than she does, leave a message on her bathroom mirror, or jot a note on an index card and stick it in her lunch or purse. Take selfies with her and use these as the backgrounds on your phone or computer.

If she's little, choose a charm bracelet for her to wear. Let her know she's "Daddy's girl." Every year on her birthday you can add a special and unique charm that tells a story about who

she is and why you think she's amazing. If she's older, a ring can
be an outward and visible reminder of your affection, esteem,
and expectations.

Week 29

APOLOGIZING

Therefore, if you are offering your gift at the altar and there remember that your brother or sister has something against you, leave your gift there in front of the altar. First go and be reconciled to them; then come and offer your gift.
—Matthew 5:23–24, NIV

I s it just me, or does it seem to you that good, old-fashioned apologizing is going the way of the 8-track player? A politician, for example, is caught with his hands in the till (or all over his young, pretty assistant). What follows is a predictable barrage of press releases and carefully orchestrated press conferences. Instead of speaking from the heart, the nervous politician reads from a prepared text, the language parsed and nuanced and tortured. Instead of mea culpa, we hear moaning about enemies. Instead of overt apologizing, we hear lots of subtle rationalizing. Instead of humility, hubris. Rationalizing is selfish. Shifting blame is cowardice.

Apologizing, on the other hand, is accepting responsibility, which is the very essence of masculinity. A real man rejects passivity, takes responsibility, and leads courageously. When a real man messes up, he steps forward and fesses up. Any coward can duck into the shadows or throw someone else under the bus. It takes a great man to step forward and admit, "That's on me. I did that. It's nobody else's fault. I was wrong. I am sorry. Let me try to make it right."

When a quarterback makes a bad throw or a point guard makes a bad pass and then taps his chest and says, "My fault," you respect him for it. It's owning up, it's taking responsibility, it's virtuous humility.

Your daughter wants and needs to see that kind of humility in *you*. Even if she's little, she intuitively knows the rightness of admitting to wrong. When she sees you do that, you become an even bigger hero in her eyes than you already are. What's more, in the process, you set the bar high for the kind of man she will want to marry: a responsible man, not an excuse-making finger-pointer.

What's involved in manly apologizing?

Recognize your failure. We're all sinners and it shouldn't be a blow to anyone's ego that we have ugly moments and bad days (even years). Ironically, Jesus said we're not really blessed until we finally realize how broken and messed up we really are (Matthew 5:3).

Determine to make things right. In the verse at the beginning of this chapter, Christ emphasizes our supreme need to be right with others. He goes so far as to say, "Even if you're in the middle of worship, if you remember you've wronged someone, stop. Leave. First go and make things right with the person you've offended. Then come back and finish worshiping." That's what God means when He tells us to pursue righteousness (see 2 Timothy 2:22); we're to make things right.

Come clean. Don't explain away your behavior. Own it. As Benjamin Franklin wisely counseled, "Never ruin an apology with an excuse."

Express authentic sorrow. Some would say "I'm sorry" is just a phrase. And what good are words against a long list of offenses? If the phrase is said mechanically or insincerely, then, yes, it's not worth saying. But spoken by a father who is grieved by the hurt he has caused, "I'm sorry" is a great start. Genuine sorrow is powerful. This is what Lynn Johnston, cartoonist of *For Better or For Worse* fame, meant when she said, "An apology is the superglue of life. It can repair just about anything."

Ask forgiveness. Jesus said the Greatest Commandment is to love God and love others (Mark 12:28–31). It stands to reason, then, that the greatest sin is to *fail* to love God and love others. When we disobey God by treating others badly, it is only fitting to ask for forgiveness. This is how we experience mercy and grace in the deepest measure.

In *Strong Father, Strong Daughters*, I wrote these words: "I have known many successful men who embody extraordinary humility. They are successful professionally, intellectually, and emotionally because they understand that life is bigger than they are. Their work and their being fit into a much larger picture. Their successes not only benefit themselves—they also help those around them. A father's humility is a gift to his daughter" (p. 78). Oftentimes that humility comes in the form of a simple, heartfelt apology.

Your daughter won't be disappointed if you apologize; she won't think you're weak. On the contrary, she'll be drawn to your honesty and the strength inherent in your humility. And she'll be learning a crucial life skill.

PRAY

God, when pride or insecurity prevent me from apologizing for my mistakes, help me to get over that, to find Your grace, and to make amends. Amen.

FLEX YOUR DAD MUSCLES

Someone has said that our offenses—until we admit and really deal with them—act as a kind of wall between us and those we've wronged. Even if time has passed and civility has returned, those unresolved and unaddressed tensions foster a lingering mistrust and distance. But when we acknowledge our faults and failures, when we apologize and seek forgiveness, they become—in an odd but real way—a bridge to the other person.

Do some personal soul-searching. Think back over your recent interactions with your daughter. Ask yourself:

- Have I used inappropriate language?
- Have I been impatient and harsh?
- Have I been a bully?
- Have I failed to practice what I preach?
- Have I failed to engage and really listen when she is talking?
- Have I been critical and demanding?
- Have I been negative and pessimistic in my outlook?
- Have I been a servant-leader to my daughter?
- Have I failed to keep a promise?
- Have I failed to be encouraging?
- Have I been insensitive to her concerns, hurts, and fears?
- Have I been emotionally absent or distant?
- Have I chosen selfish pursuits instead of time with her?

- Have I missed important events because of disordered priorities?
- Have I reacted out of anger when under pressure or frustrated?

If as you ponder that list, you realize you have caused harm or hurt feelings in thought, word, or deed, then take action. You might need to make an "Apology Tour." That's okay. We need more men and fathers like that.

Week 30

Biting Your Tongue

Too much talk leads to sin.
Be sensible and keep your mouth shut.
—Proverbs 10:19, NLT

T hose of us who write and do a lot of speaking know the sobering wisdom of Solomon's words. The more you talk, the more likely you are to end up saying something you'll regret.

Pastor and author Charlie Shedd tells a story in his bestselling book *Letters to Karen* about a young couple that came to him once for marriage counseling. It seems the woman had freckles all over her face—the source of tremendous insecurity since her early teen years. Her husband had always insisted he was crazy about her freckles, until one night during a heated argument, he shouted angrily, "I never did like your darned old freckles anyway!" As you might guess, a thousand apologies could not undo the damage. Nor did they erase the pernicious little question in her mind: *When was he really telling the truth?*

There is no taking back our words. You can almost always come back later and say what you need to say. You can't go back and un-say things. Thus this additional reminder/encouragement from Solomon: "The words of the reckless pierce like swords, but the tongue of the wise brings healing" (Proverbs 12:18, NIV).

What's involved in cultivating the skill of "biting your tongue"?

Listening. In the old *All in the Family* TV show, Archie, the loud, bigoted patriarch of the dysfunctional little Bunker family, would often look with disdain at his chattering wife and bark, "Stifle!" What a rude thing to say to another person (but what a wise bit of counsel to give yourself). With your daughter, it's good to stifle the urge to interrupt and dump a truckload of unsolicited advice. Instead of lecturing, it's far better to sit, focus, pay careful attention, and ask a lot of clarifying questions.

In *Strong Fathers, Strong Daughters*, I tell the story of Ainsley, a Midwestern girl who went to college in the Ivy League. She had a great first year. But during her second year something shifted inside her, and the school ended up kicking her out.

All during the long drive home, Ainsley fretted over how her parents would react. As feared, her mother lit in to her, shouting, shaming, and lecturing. Her father, however, kept what disappointment he felt to himself. He listened. He waited. His only whispered words were "Are you all right?" All these years later, Ainsley points to her father's gentle, quiet response that night as a breakthrough moment in her life and in their relationship.

Both men and women tend to think we can best effect change by powering up in tense situations, then delivering strong words in a loud and stern tone of voice. Sometimes we get the results we want through such verbal force. But I have seen that greater power is often found in biting your tongue and quietly listening first. I love the words of James Dent, which are especially powerful for parents: "As you go through life you are going to have many opportunities to keep your mouth shut. Take advantage of all of them."

Pondering. What do you do when you encounter a problem at work? My guess is you gather information. Then you spend time analyzing and processing that data. Maybe you bring others into the loop to help you assess and come up with a solution.

Why would we do anything less as a parent? When presented with a hard or confusing situation involving your daughter, don't immediately open the verbal floodgates. Spend some time gathering facts. Then sit down with your wife (or ex-wife) and think through the best possible response. **Waiting.** "There is a time for everything, and a season for every activity under the heavens…a time to be silent and a time to speak" (Ecclesiastes 3:1, 7, NIV). Sometimes it's not the right time for you to talk, because you're too worked up. Or maybe *you're* calm and rational, but your daughter isn't in the right frame of mind to listen—meaning, any words on your part in such a tense moment would just be wasted. Sometimes, by waiting, by biting your tongue and letting your daughter vent, she hits upon a solution to her own problem. This is a good thing—a necessary part of the maturation process. Good things, as the old saying goes, come to those who wait. So wait to see what she will do. Wait for the right time to speak. How will you know when it's the right time?

Praying. Ask for divine wisdom. Ask the Spirit of God to give you clarity to understand—the situation, your daughter's needs, your own responsibility, the best way forward. Ask for a right attitude—to be motivated not by a desire to punish or humiliate or "put her in her place" but by love. Pray for a heart that seeks not to be right, or vindicated, but your daughter's best. Pray for sensitivity to choose exactly the right words. Pray for gentleness and courage in saying them. Here's a great psalm to pray: "Let the words of my mouth and the meditation of my heart be acceptable in your sight, O LORD, my rock and my Redeemer" (Psalms 19:14, NASB). A second is this: "Take control of what I say, O LORD, and guard my lips" (Psalms 141:3, NLT).

Speaking. The Gospel of John begins with a description of Christ, saying He was "full of grace and truth" (John 1:14, NASB). What a beautiful measuring stick for our own words. When you do feel prompted to end your God-led, self-imposed silence, ask: *Are my thoughts and words honest and are they loving?* Truthfulness and tenderness should always be our goal. When speaking, speak carefully, gently, and thoughtfully. Consciously follow the guideline of the apostle Paul, who said our words should always "give grace to those who hear" (Ephesians 4:29, ESV).

Dads who follow these guidelines have less to go back and apologize for. When you start listening more and talking less, your daughter will feel loved and heard. She will feel valued. And she will be more inclined to perk up on those occasions when you do open your mouth.

Remember: you will never regret the thoughtless words you didn't say.

PRAY

God, I'm guilty. When my daughter starts babbling and saying silly or foolish things, my tendency is either to tune her out or to give her an earful. Forgive my habit of lecturing and chiding. Help me to implement the truths I've read here. I want to become more adept at learning to bite my tongue. Instead of reacting in a knee-jerk way, I want to be responsive and thoughtful. I ask for Your help. Amen.

FLEX YOUR DAD MUSCLES

If your daughter is young (nine or under), do a silly exercise with her. Tell her you are going to play the talking and listening game. Tell her she gets to put tape over your mouth, and she gets to do all the talking for ten whole minutes. Explain that she can talk about whatever she wants and you won't say a word. You'll only promise to listen and pay attention.

If your daughter is older (ten or over), see if you can get her to engage around some questions like:

- What's your biggest worry right now?
- What things in life make it hard for you to trust God?
- What do you feel is the biggest thing missing from your life?
- Why do you think God put you on this earth?
- If you could go back and relive any one day of your life, what day would that be and why?
- What do you think "true love" looks like? How will you know when you've met "Mr. Right"?
- What's one thing you wish you could change about our family?
- Do you pray? If so, what kinds of things do you pray for?

Remember, this is not a time for you to pontificate or correct. This is a time for you to "stifle" the urge to talk and to practice the skill of listening. Take good mental notes. This exercise is likely to open doors to some great conversations down the road.

Week 31

COACHING

For the Lord takes delight in his people;
he crowns the humble with victory.
—Psalms 149:4, NIV

I f coaching is the art of training and preparing another person in order to bring out that individual's best, then in a real sense dads are coaches to their kids.

A coach has to wear a lot of hats. He is part salesman and motivator, part tactician and disciplinarian. Coaching has a technical aspect—that is, the teaching of skills. But it also involves interpersonal and psychological aspects as well. Lou Holtz has said, "I'd say handling people is the most important thing you can do as a coach."

The world of sports has demonstrated time and again that the best coaches are those who know their players' strengths and weaknesses, who gain their trust, who equip them to succeed, who put them in a position to do so, and who constantly convey the positive message, "I believe in you. You can do this." As the great Don Shula once said, "My responsibility is leadership, and the minute I get negative, that is going to have an influence on my team."

In The 12 Principles of Raising Great Kids from The Strong Parent Project online program, I talk about the three essential questions that every child needs answered: (1) What do you believe about me? (2) How do you feel about me? (3) What are your hopes for me?

These are exactly the kinds of questions a good coach answers for his players.

"What do you believe about me?" Consider this sobering truth: every time your daughter interacts with you, she leaves your presence either feeling better or worse about who she is. When you speak to your daughter or when she talks to you, she studies your face, listens to your tone of voice, and pays close attention to your body language. Then she interprets all that and concludes: *what I am saying is worthwhile* or *my dad thinks my words and ideas are unimportant.*

Let's say you ask your daughter a question about school and she begins to reply, but then you take a phone call or respond to a text while she is talking. What does your daughter assume? That her answer is insignificant to you. If you do this once or twice, it's not a big deal, but if you do it on a regular basis, your daughter will conclude: *my father doesn't believe I matter.*

Do you believe in me? Do you believe I'm capable? Do you believe I have what it takes? Do you believe I'm attractive? Do you believe I have something to offer? Do you believe I'm worth fighting for? These are the questions that your daughter is asking. How you answer these questions both verbally and nonverbally will change who she becomes. She won't find the answers (at least not the right answers) on the soccer field, in the classroom, or on some stage. She will get the real answers she needs and wants when she is face to face with you. She will receive them in the common moments of a normal day when the two of you are doing nothing special at all.

"**How do you feel about me?**" Answering this question is tricky. It isn't really about how you feel; it is about what your daughter *believes* you feel about her.

I love the way one father answered this question for his daughter. Rose was attending a good school and playing soccer. She was a talented musician. But something inside her shifted when she turned fourteen. She changed friends, got "tatted up," started skipping school, and pulled away from her parents. Sullen and rebellious, Rose was not exactly fun to be around. In desperation her father came to me for help. I suggested, "Why don't you take her away for a long weekend?" Even though Rose wasn't speaking to him at the time, he agreed to give it a try. He took her canoeing.

That first day she refused to say a word. His response was to patiently paddle and, that evening, to gently ask for her help in pitching the tent. The second day, she gave terse answers to his questions. He quietly paddled their canoe. The third day Rose erupted in anger. She screamed at her father and called him names. He resisted the urge to react in kind. The fourth day, Rose began to cry, wailing, "You don't care about me! You and Mom never pay attention to me. You only want me to 'look good' in front of your friends. You're a terrible parent!"

It was not a good trip—until the fifth day. That's when Rose and her father actually connected. They talked and cried together. Though the ensuing months were really hard, the camping trip was a catalyst for transforming their relationship and changing Rose's future.

How? During those five days, Rose's father answered a crucial question for her. His patient actions made clear to her that there was nothing she could do to shake his love for her. Through his actions, he communicated to his daughter, "Even when you act horribly, I still want your company." That was it. It brings to mind what legendary football coach Amos Alonzo Stagg once said: "You must love your [players] to get the most out of them and do the most for them. I have worked with boys whom I haven't admired, but I have loved them just the same. Love has dominated my coaching career." Love is what needs to dominate a father's role as well.

"**What are your hopes for me?**" Great coaches (and great fathers) have a vision. That is, they talk in hopeful terms about the future. They take the long view about what their team is becoming. When asked what kind of team he had, Coach Stagg used to say he would know in twenty years— "When I find out how many doctors and lawyers and good husbands and good citizens have come off of my team."

That's what a good coach does. He whets his players' appetite by being positive and having a vision for the future. His affirmation gives them a reason to train, to keep trying, to get better. Your daughter needs to hear you say, "I am so proud of you and I believe in you. The sky is the limit for you."

Maybe you find it hard to sense, much less pass on, such hope because your own father never said such things to you. Here is what I know: ultimate hope is grounded in the extraordinary fact that God absolutely adores you. It doesn't matter what you've done or where you've been, God is a good and perfect Father. He delights in His children. Receiving this love from God is essential if you ever hope to love your own children in a healthy way.

PRAY

God, make me sensitive today to small but significant ways in which I can prepare my daughter for success. Help me to teach her through encouragement and love. Amen.

FLEX YOUR DAD MUSCLES

While it's fresh on your mind, write your daughter a list of five to ten things you believe about her (for example, I believe you are really smart—God has given you a good mind. I believe you have the potential to influence your friends in good ways). Leave it in a place where she'll be sure to see it.

Sometime tomorrow sit down with her and pour out your heart. By that, I mean tell her how you love her or just talk about how you felt the day she was born. Or tell her about a time your heart was so full of love for her you thought you might burst.

Later, you might want to make a list of your hopes for her. Don't program her life (I hope you will go to State U. and pledge Tri Kappa like your mom and become a doctor like your dear old dad). Rather, share more general hopes (I hope you will save sex for marriage. I hope you will marry a strong man who is humble and a servant to others. I hope you will pursue your dreams).

CONNECTING

The purposes of a person's heart are deep waters,
but one who has insight draws them out.

—Proverbs 20:5, NIV

K ing Solomon describes the human heart as being full of beauty and mystery, but we need insightful people to draw that beauty and mystery out. That's what great novelists, playwrights, and screenwriters do. And it is what great friends, mentors, and family members in our own lives can do as well.

As a father, part of your job description is to draw out the best from your children, to help them find their talents, nurture their skills, develop their character. You need to connect with them in a profound way, as only a father can.

As a wife and mother and grandmother, and with over thirty years of experience as a pediatrician, I've seen over and over again that one of the things that makes a good father is a commitment to connect with his daughter. He doesn't leave it all to mom, thinking, "Well, they're women, they understand each other," or leave his daughter to grow up on her own without his "interference." No, the best fathers provide what their daughters desperately want—a connection to his authority and leadership.

Here's how:

Enter her world. Take a few moments to ask yourself: *What is it like to be my daughter? What is her school experience like? What music does she enjoy? Who are her friends? What do they do when they're together?* Granted, you might not know all the answers—and you certainly don't want your daughter to think you are spying or prying. But the point is that you need to have both an imaginative and a real connection to your daughter's world. If you have backed out because of the cultural pressure to "give your kids more space, and fewer rules and limits," you need to muster the courage to reenter her world. She needs you. She wants to connect with you more than you realize.

Time your conversations well. You can't simply fit your daughter into the empty spaces in your schedule. Just because you're alert at 6:30 a.m. and have a few minutes before work doesn't mean that's the best time for her. Good fathers figure out when their kids are most inclined to open up. Evenings are optimal for most (especially during the teenage years). Connecting with your daughter might require you to stay up an extra hour at night when she's alone and her homework is done. You might find she's less guarded and more receptive to simple questions about her life then.

Sit down. In our busy, multitasking culture, to stop and pull up a chair communicates volumes: *I am here. I want to be with you. I want to hear your heart.*

Ask personal questions. Girls think about themselves constantly (and this self-obsession goes into overdrive during adolescence). One of the best ways to connect with your daughter is to ask her open-ended questions that require more than a yes or no answer about herself. Here are some good starters:

- What would you say is the best book you've ever read?
- What's the worst food you've ever tasted?

- On a scale of one to ten, how would you rate yourself as a dancer, a singer, an artist, a writer?
- Do you have a lot of dreams in your sleep? About what?
- If you were stranded on a desert island with only three possessions, what would you want to have with you?
- What friend makes you laugh the hardest?
- What would be your perfect day?
- What's the best age to get married?
- What's something that kids at school do that bugs you?
- What was the best thing that happened to you today?

When your daughter seems more relaxed and chatty, you can go deeper:

- What's the most stressful thing in your life right now?
- Of all your accomplishments, what are you proudest of?
- What's something you'd like to do if you had a bit more courage?

Make eye contact. Turn off the TV, put down your phone or tablet or book or magazine. As she talks, look her in the eyes. Eye contact is intimate. It says, *I want to connect with you.*

Resist the urge to interrupt. I come from a family of talkers (which is fine by me because I love to listen). But what frustrates me to no end is the way members of my family constantly interrupt each other. I want to hear the end of the sentence, the rest of the story.

When you interrupt your daughter (or anyone else, for that matter), you're essentially communicating, *I don't really care to hear the rest of what you're saying because either (a) it's not that interesting, or (b) I completely dismiss what you're saying, or (c) what I want to say is more important.* Since kids are more emotionally sensitive, resist the urge to jump in and correct or rebut. Bite your tongue. It will pay off, I promise.

When your daughter senses you sincerely want to connect with her, and when you give her the opportunity to be heard, she will reveal a lot about herself: her likes and dislikes, deepest desires, greatest hopes, biggest dreams, and scariest fears.

As I wrote in my book *Your Kids at Risk: How Teen Sex Threatens Our Sons and Daughters*, "Communication opens the door for relationships. Intimacy cements them together. A psychologist friend of mine once explained intimacy in this way. 'Intimacy means "INTO-ME-SEE."' How simple and true" (p. 205).

PRAY

God, I want to thank You again for my daughter. She is precious to me. Solomon was right: she is also like deep waters. I need extra wisdom and insight to draw out the plans and hopes and hurts of her heart. Grant that I might connect with her in an ever-deepening way. Amen.

FLEX YOUR DAD MUSCLES

Make the effort to have at least two connecting conversations with your daughter this week. When you do, sit down, maintain eye contact, ask questions, and then keep your mouth closed and listen while she talks. Rather than give your opinion or go into "fix-it mode" right away, draw her out further with questions that give her an opportunity to share more of her thoughts and feelings.

Ask any nonjudgmental question you can think to ask—so long as it comes from a place of genuine curiosity. Otherwise, sit back, focus, maintain eye contact, and listen. Your daughter will be so thrown off and so thrilled that you are making the effort to hear her, she will open up again and again. You will have some great conversations and build a much stronger connection with your daughter.

Week 33

DISCIPLINE

Discipline your children, for in that there is hope;
do not be a willing party to their death.
—Proverbs 19:18, NIV

rue confession: when I was raising my children, I hated disciplining them. I wanted my kids to like me and enjoy being with me. And discipline felt, well, antithetical to being a nice parent.

This aversion to discipline wasn't unique to me. The majority of parents I've observed over the years are reluctant to administer necessary discipline to their children. Why is this? There are probably a hundred reasons, but let me list just four:

1. *Discipline is unpleasant.* Discipline is almost always the end result of tension and conflict. And who likes that?
2. *Discipline takes time.* It's disruptive. Addressing misbehavior means having to stop what you're doing. It's far easier to look the other way or try to bark your kids in line with an empty threat or two.
3. *Discipline is grueling.* Sometimes we can have three or four confrontations with our kids—and that's just before breakfast.

4. *Discipline can seem "mean."* Many of us feel this way because we experienced harsh correction, even abuse, from our own parents. Here's the important distinction: discipline is not punishing our children; it is teaching them. Good and effective discipline is never, ever cruel. What *is* cruel, according to the verse above, is *not* disciplining—not teaching and training—our kids.

In the Bible, we read the sad story of Adonijah. The fourth son of King David, Adonijah was extremely handsome, and also filled with a lust for power. When David was elderly, Adonijah decided to stage a brazen coup and wrest the throne from his father, even though David had promised that Solomon would be Israel's next king.

Scripture notes of Adonijah that "His father, King David, had never disciplined him at any time, even by asking, 'Why are you doing that?'" (1 Kings 1:6, NLT). In other words, David—whether due to royal distractions or weariness or misplaced priorities—never called Adonijah's behavior into question. He never worked to instill in his son the indispensable quality of self-control. The result: Adonijah was self-centered to the point of treachery and betrayal, and he ended badly—dying violently at the hands of his half-brother Solomon. For all we know, it was this tragic incident that prompted Solomon to challenge fathers: "Discipline your children, for in that there is hope; do not be a willing party to their death" (Proverbs 19:18, NIV).

Effective discipline can make children more respectful and better mannered, but the real point is to teach them self-control.

Self-control is indispensable; something you will find in any person who is happy and successful; and one of the best protections against life's pitfalls.

The self-controlled husband has learned not to blurt out every thought that comes into his mind during a marital spat. The self-controlled businessman has disciplined himself to listen attentively and respond quickly to the needs of his customers and employees. The self-controlled athlete has relentlessly trained his body through constant practice to respond to the demands of elite competition.

People who don't have self-control are heading for trouble—emotional, financial, and in every other way.

You instill self-control in your children, through discipline, by being firm and consistent. Start early, if you can, and keep at it. Making sure your daughter does her homework well and on time, every night, is one good place to start.

As she grows older, you can give her more freedom in direct proportion to her self-control and her growing ability to make mature decisions. This is scary, but necessary. Sadly, many dads do just the opposite. As their daughters get older, they clamp down. Resist this urge. Remember that your job description is to teach your daughter to monitor her own life and behavior.

Dad, please don't shrink from this critical job. Own your authority. You have been chosen by God to be your daughter's dad. If you don't step up, someone else will, someone who doesn't love her like you do.

The fact is, daughters might fuss and fume on the surface, but they respect their fathers for caring enough about them to discipline them. A father's authority makes a daughter feel secure. A father who lets his daughter run wild, leaves his daughter looking for security elsewhere— perhaps with a group of friends or a boyfriend you might not like.

Be sure of this: committing to discipline will be unpleasant. It will take time and even threaten to wear you out. On occasion, your daughter will try to make you feel like a big "meanie" for grounding her or taking away privileges. Shake it off. Don't give up. Stay at it. The payoff will be an amazing young woman who can control herself. And because of that, you will have put her on a path that leads to success and bypasses unnecessary pain in life.

PRAY

God, I want to be this kind of dad. I want to take seriously my calling to help my daughter learn the quality of self-control. When I get discouraged or start to shirk my responsibility, give me the grace to keep doing what I know is right. Amen.

FLEX YOUR DAD MUSCLES

Here are some key truths about discipline to remember:

- Self-control is the essence of discipline. Question for myself: Do I exhibit self-control?
- My daughter cannot succeed in school, relationships, or life if she does not learn self-control.
- Discipline is for my daughter's ultimate benefit, not mine.
- I set the rules, not my daughter. Having firm guidelines makes her feel safe, secure, and loved. A life without rules is frightening.
- Saying no is a gift to my daughter. Do I do this enough?
- I will apply discipline only when necessary—not all childish mistakes or behaviors need corrective discipline.

- Discipline is not yelling; it is calmly applying consequences to inappropriate, rebellious actions.
- Good discipline takes time, and my daughter will need to be reminded of the rules repeatedly. Repetition is not a sign of failure. My daughter is a work in progress.

Pick your battles. It's easy to get discouraged if you try to squash a bunch of misbehaviors at once. Here's an approach that yields better results:

- Pick *one* behavior that your daughter does that really bugs you.
- When you're calm, inform her that this behavior will no longer be tolerated in your home. Spell out the consequences if she does it again.
- Ask her if she has questions.
- Then, get ready. She will throw the gauntlet down. She wants to know if you are serious.
- Realize: you *must* win the battle.
- It might take weeks of reinforcing your stated consequences. But hang in there. Don't go soft.
- Once she realizes who the boss is, it will be easier to modify her behavior in other areas.

GETTING OFF THE CRAZY TRAIN

There is a way that seems right to a man,
but its end is the way to death.
—Proverbs 14:12, ESV

Perhaps you've heard me reference the "Crazy Train." Many parents find themselves stuck on it. The "Crazy Train" is a cultural bullet train knocking down everything in its path. Printed on its side is the inscription: "Parents have to make their children happy and successful 24/7."

I have been there myself. I've ridden more than a few miles on this awful express. Clearly, the parents who buy a ticket on this runaway railroad put immense pressure on themselves and end up having enormous expectations for their kids. The results are never pretty.

"Crazy Train" parents do whatever it takes to push and prod and drive their children to succeed. That's the goal: success (*success* being defined as a smart, attractive, accomplished, connected kid who excels in whatever she does).

To this end, a "Crazy Train" mom or dad or couple feels an inordinate responsibility to make sure their daughter gets the best (and only the best) of everything: enrollment in the best college-prep schools, tutors, lessons of all kinds, extreme dietary oversight, exotic vacations and summer camp experiences, sought-after trainers and coaches for their athletic pursuits, closets full of the top clothing brands, entrance into the "right" social circles, and ultimately acceptance to an elite college.

For the parents, there's pressure to work extra-long hours, often in stressful jobs (how else to afford these expensive perks and goals?). It also means obsessively investigating every controversial aspect of being a parent—from immunizations to day care to you name it.

Now factor in the daily necessities of life: carpool, team sports (often with multiple kids having games and practices weekly), doctor appointments, music lessons, homework, laundry, cooking, cleaning, household chores, church activities, social events, a personal exercise regimen. (Whew! Are you worn out yet?)

As if this weren't enough, occasionally a "Crazy Train" parent feels the need to double as a full-fledged helicopter parent, fretting over (and trying to manage and control) *every* little detail of his or her child's life.

By this point, life has ceased to be a wild miracle, an amazing gift from God, something to be cherished. Now the moments and days are just something to be endured and conquered. In their obsession to get to that magical place called "success," such parents (and their kids) miss the loveliness of the trip itself.

Are you surprised that huge numbers of parents (maybe most) feel like life is dragging them around by the ankles? Do you scratch your head at the fact that so many moms and dads exist in a kind of perpetual state of exhaustion? Maybe you, like them, feel frantic all through your days and defeated at the end of those days.

Is it any wonder that so many of the girls I see in my practice are depressed or suffer from anxiety disorders? The "Crazy Train" might *seem* like it's the only way to success and the good life, but as Solomon grimly noted in the verse at the beginning of this chapter, sometimes the path that everybody insists is the right, best one actually takes you to the last place you'd ever want to go.

If this is you, if you're a passenger on the "Crazy Train," I've got bad news and good news. First, the bad news: you've made a mistake. Instead of making an obsessive effort to have your daughter excel at academics and sports, you should focus on her heart and spirit—that's the part of her that defines who she is and makes you love her.

Now the good news: you can get off the "Crazy Train." There's a better way to raise a daughter. Isaiah 30 records the Jewish prophet speaking God's words to a nation of weary, jaded people. The ancient Israelites weren't experiencing the good life that God desired for them. In fact, they hadn't known such a life for a long, long time. This prompted Isaiah to say, "For thus the Lord GOD, the Holy One of Israel, has said, 'In repentance and rest you will be saved, in quietness and trust is your strength'" (Isaiah 30:15, NASB).

What is *repentance*? It means recognizing that you made a mistake (or sinned) and that you're committed to changing that and doing right. And part of doing right means spending more time praying (which requires quiet and focus) and trusting God (Who gives rest to our weariness).

God's plan for your daughter is surely more than about getting her into an Ivy League school or winning a high school championship softball game (as nice as those things might be). God is interested in your daughter's soul. And that should be your focus as well.

Obviously it's not wrong to want good things for your child. But when you pursue those things so intently that your lives becomes one continuous stress test, that's a sign you've gone too far. When your daughter's credentials become more important to you than her character, you've just bought a ticket for the "Crazy Train."

Don't make that mistake. You can be a great dad and *not* live like this. In fact, when you get off the crazy train and pay attention to the things that really matter, you'll find that you actually have a happier, healthier, better life—and a closer relationship with your daughter based on who she is rather than what she's done.

PRAY

God, I pray that you might grant me the courage and the wisdom to raise my daughter the right way, with a joyful eye on her as an individual, remembering that she is a unique eternal soul, not a catalogue of worldly accomplishments. Amen.

FLEX YOUR DAD MUSCLES

Take an inventory of your family's activities and how many hours a week you spend on them. Then ask yourself:

- Do my wife and I and our kids have enough downtime?
- Am I allowing my daughter to enjoy her childhood, her teen years?
- Which activities are most important to us? Which are the least important to us? Are they important to us for the right reasons? And which would we all, if we're honest, rather skip?

KEEPING YOUR EYE ON THE BALL

To have a fool for a child brings grief;
there is no joy for the parent of a godless fool.
—Proverbs 17:21, NIV

I n my book *Teens at Risk: How Teen Sex Threatens Our Sons and Daughters*, I tell the story of Myra. The moment I met her and her parents, I knew their home situation was critical.

"I just don't know what to do with her...she's out of control," her dad blurted out. What followed was a sad but typical story. In her early teens, Myra's restlessness had led her parents to let her do pretty much what she wanted. She went to parties with older kids. She dated older boys. The consequences were predictable: Myra ended up pregnant (though before informing her parents, she procured an abortion). Afterward, her rebellion continued—and so did her parents' leniency. They figured that if they tried to rein her in, she'd only pull away more.

The decision by Myra's parents to schedule an appointment with me had been triggered by a fear that their daughter might be pregnant *again*. As her parents talked, Myra was stiff, her countenance angry. I couldn't tell if she might suddenly start screaming or sobbing.

Myra wasn't pregnant. But she did have an STD. I treated her and recommended a good family counselor. I can report that in time, Myra got better and her relationship with her parents healed. Still, it was a harrowing journey.

Myra's parents made one huge mistake. They gave their daughter far too much freedom long before she was ready to handle it.

It's easy to do. As parents, we want our kids to like us. We don't want to come across as sticks in the mud or party poopers. But getting your daughter to like you or think you're cool is not the job description of a father. You are there to protect her, guide her, teach her, and discipline her. Only when she consistently demonstrates maturity and responsibility should your start giving her more freedom.

Some parents, of course, lean too far the other way. They institute a million rules and demand strict observance. Too often the result is a child who complies *only so long as she is being monitored and threatened with dire consequences.* When she leaves home: she goes wild.

A strong father is a reflective father who asks himself about *why* his daughter might be misbehaving, *how* he can prepare her for adulthood, *what* projects he can give her to teach her responsibility, and *who* is the one she is to live for and has to answer to (God).

The proverb with which I started this chapter is worth mulling over. It says, "There is no joy for the parent of a godless fool." The implication, however, is that for the parent of a godly, wise young daughter, there is great joy.

This is why you, as her dad, have to keep your eye on the ball, the objective. When your daughter took those first wobbly steps, it was a hint, a foreshadowing, of how she will eventually walk out of your home into her own independent adult life.

Experienced dads will tell you: blink a few times, and your baby's suddenly walking into her first grade classroom. A few more flips of the calendar, and she's walking out onto the soccer field or volleyball court.

Before you can even catch your breath, she's walking out the front door to drive herself to school for the first time. Next thing you know, it's the glimpse of her in your rearview mirror as she walks back into her freshman dorm. Then in a blurry flash, you are walking her down the aisle to give her away to the man who will assume the role of loving and leading her.

Everything you do as a father is pointed toward this. You're not trying to be a buddy—or a prison warden. Your job is to prepare your daughter for life.

Along the way, you'll be thrown a few curves, but here's how to keep your eye on the ball:

Realize. Her growing sense of independence (starting in puberty) isn't just nerve-racking to you; it's unsettling for your daughter. That's why at fifteen, she might be giggling about boys and putting on makeup one moment, and sleeping with her favorite childhood stuffed animal the next. Realize the challenges she faces in growing up.

Redefine. As she grows more independent, you'll also find that she grows more absent, spending less time at home and more time with her friends. She might balk at family vacations and not want to be seen with you in public. She might compare you unfavorably to so-and-so's parents. She might skip chores, break curfew, talk back (more than she previously did), and ask for more freedom. What she's really asking is "How far can I go?" As her father, you need to be engaged, to understand your daughter's level of maturity, to say no when necessary, and yes when she's deserving of more latitude. Luckily, it's a gradual process. A strong father knows that his relationship with his daughter will be redefined as she grows older—it will always be essential, but in different ways.

Relinquish. Parents hate this thought, but being a parent is a long process of letting go. The challenge for dads is to find safer ways for daughters to exert their independence. Offer smaller freedoms—the freedom to choose her own clothes (within reason), hairstyles, the way she decorates her room—before moving to bigger ones—going on dates, taking a job, opening a checking account, perhaps even taking responsibility for a car. As her dad, help her find appropriate ways to become independent while maintaining appropriate boundaries.

Remember, *rules and boundaries make her feel loved.* So don't be afraid to act like a dad in her best interests. But also accept that as she grows more mature, you will necessarily, gradually be relinquishing control of her life.

Keep your eye on the ball. In the end, you want a daughter who will be a strong, independent, moral adult.

PRAY

God, help me to find the right balance between control and freedom in raising my daughter. I pray for Your guidance as the balance changes. I pray to remember that my goal as a father is not to raise a child, but an adult of strong character. Amen.

FLEX YOUR DAD MUSCLES

A final word of caution: when your daughter breaks clearly stated, nonnegotiable rules (and feisty teenage girls will break them just to test your reaction), you must enforce serious consequences. I recommend that all such rules focus on personal safety and respect for others. For instance, underage drinking (especially mixed with driving) is illegal and can kill, so this is an obvious, nonnegotiable rule. Speeding is another good example. At our house, if a kid got a speeding ticket, driving privileges were taken away for a predetermined period of time, say three to six months, depending on the child's age. Such rules and enforced consequences are critical to our teens. The family has to be the place where your daughter learns how rules and consequences work.

Week 36

LEADING

And David shepherded them with integrity of heart;
with skillful hands he led them.
—Psalms 78:72, NIV

L eadership is surely one of the hottest topics around. There's no end
to new books discussing the latest theories, principles, and case
studies relating to good leadership. There's no shortage of seminars
that offer the latest leadership tips and techniques. But what exactly *is*
leadership? And what does it mean for a father to lead his family and lead
his daughter well?

John Maxwell has said, "Leadership is influence—nothing more, nothing
less." General Colin Powell has asserted, "Leadership is solving problems."
According to Susan Ascher (founder, president, and CEO of SusanAscher.
com), "A leader is a person who takes you where you will not go alone."

All these definitions are solid; but for fathers, the description of King David
in Psalms 78:72 is best. A father needs to be a good shepherd, he needs to have
integrity of heart, he needs skillful hands, and he needs to be a true leader.

A good shepherd. A shepherd not only guides his sheep, he feeds them,
he calms them, and he keeps them safe from predators. A father is like a
shepherd; your family is your flock.

In *Strong Fathers, Strong Daughters*, I noted how little girls want and need to be shepherded by their dads. "When your daughter is born, she recognizes your voice as deeper than her mother's. As a toddler, she looks up at your enormous frame and realizes that you are big, smart, and tough. In her grade school years, she instinctively turns to you for direction" (p. 30). When your daughter becomes a teenager, your role as a shepherd becomes more difficult, but it's just as necessary.

Your daughter still wants a shepherd; she still desperately needs you to be the authority figure in her life—even if she screams against it. That scream is simply a test: to see how much you really care.

My own father was extremely protective of me—even during my college years—and I chafed against it. But I now appreciate that he was a good and diligent shepherd and that his strong guidance kept me out of trouble and made me feel loved and secure.

Integrity of heart. Girls want their dads to be men of high character; and they are more obedient to fathers they feel they can trust and respect.

This was true in the case of Mindy (see *Strong Fathers, Strong Daughters*, pp. 43–46). She watched in awe as her father faithfully cared for her mother following a devastating automobile wreck. His patience, perseverance, and faith, his devotion to his marriage vows and his family, earned him true hero status in Mindy's eyes.

Strong character justifies, like nothing else, your role as a father, because that, in your daughter's eyes, is what a father is supposed to be: a man of pure and strong heart. When she sees that in action, she loves it.

Skillful hands. Leadership is a skill, and like most stills, it's something that can be learned and made better through practice and experience.

When you read books like this one, or take online courses like The 12 Principles of Raising Great Kids from The Strong Parent Project online program, or participate in video studies for men like *33: The Series*, you demonstrate a commitment to better lead your family.

Never neglect to improve your leadership skills, remembering that all leadership involves character, understanding, and action.

True leadership. Our world is filled with leaders who talk brashly and bully their underlings. Jesus rejected this kind of "leadership." He said, "You know that the rulers of the Gentiles lord it over them, and their high officials exercise authority over them. Not so with you. Instead, whoever wants to become great among you must be your servant, and whoever wants to be first must be your slave—just as the Son of Man did not come to be served, but to serve, and to give his life as a ransom for many" (Matthew 20:25–28, NIV).

This is the most important principle of all: you lead your daughter best by serving her.

As long as you exercise your God-given authority with the care and integrity it deserves, you will have your daughter's respect. She will test you constantly, but if you shepherd her with gentleness and love, she will look to you for guidance. The moment you stop shepherding your daughter, she'll look for someone else to take your place, someone who might not have your same good intentions.

Don't let that happen.

I'll close with these stirring words from Ralph Waldo Emerson: "The characteristic of a genuine heroism is its persistency. All men have wandering impulses, fits and starts of generosity. But when you have resolved to be great, abide by yourself, and do not weakly try to reconcile yourself with the world. The heroic cannot be the common, nor the common the heroic."

PRAY

God, I pray that through Your grace I might develop the strength, courage, and character to become a true servant-leader. Amen.

FLEX YOUR DAD MUSCLES

Do an experiment in leading your daughter. Sit down with her and agree on a secret plan for doing something sweet for a family member. Maybe you'll decide to cook and serve your wife's favorite meal. Or maybe you'll clean out and wash and wax her big brother's car. Listen to her suggestions. Then decide on a clear course of action. Make sure you communicate it well to your daughter.

As you begin, give her a task to do (making sure you set her up for success by not giving her a responsibility she can't handle). Then work with her side-by-side and lead her with excellence. Give her encouragement and constructive advice. Show her tricks as you go. Enjoy just being with her. Laugh and talk together. Talk about the importance of serving. Praise her for a job well done.

Make it your goal to be the kind of leader she will always want to follow.

LIKING

I long to see you, that I may be filled with joy.
—2 Timothy 1:4, esv

A father named Bill recently confessed:

What has happened to my daughter? Abbie has always been a sweet, caring, respectful little girl—just a delight to be with. But now that she's 12, she's like a totally different kid. Always moody. Sullen. Angry. She disappears into her room for hours at a time. She treats her mother horribly. When I try to engage her, she looks at me with disgust. She used to sit in my lap and watch games with me, come out in my shop while I piddled around. Now she doesn't want to have anything to do with me. If I suggest doing something together, she either rolls her eyes or makes snarky comments under her breath.

I feel guilty saying this, but, honestly, I don't really like her anymore. I know that's a terrible thing to admit, but I don't. Isn't that something? A father who doesn't even like his own flesh and blood? But Abbie's become a pill! A selfish little diva. Sometimes it's all I can do not to just go off on her.

I know a lot of dads who can relate to Bill's plight. Here's the truth: kids (especially as they move into the teenage years) aren't always likable. They can be selfish and mean, bitter and surly. I was a physician for a halfway house for girls. I spent hundreds of hours with victims of sexual, physical, and emotional abuse. They would show up in my office like wounded, cornered alley cats. It wasn't easy in the midst of their wild, vulgar, obnoxious rants to muster up compassion and see through the angry facades to the hurting, depressed girls underneath. But if they were ever going to be helped, I had to connect with them. That meant gaining their trust. And that involved me making them feel liked and accepted. I won't lie. It is tough to like someone who seems to be doing his or her best to be unlikable.

As Bill's experience attests, this isn't only something true of street kids or runaways. Even "good" kids from "normal" homes can sometimes be hard to like. When your daughter is moody or surly, walled off or hostile, it's easy to want to throw up your hands and think, *I quit. What's the use?* Truth be told, sometimes liking your own child is difficult.

And yet, if your daughter is convinced you like her, she'll want to connect with you. If she senses your constant disapproval or that your affection is reluctant, forced, or faked, she will shut you out. This is why it's crucial to let her know that you like the person she is.

This doesn't, of course, mean that you have to like everything she does or agree with everything she says. Your daughter can deal with your disapproval so long as she knows that you accept her and love her, despite her flaws and your disagreements.

So what's a father like Bill—a father of a disrespectful, smart-mouthed daughter—to do? Here's how I answered that question in my book *Your Kids at Risk: How Teen Sex Threatens Our Sons and Daughters*: "The key to liking unlikable teens lies in refusing to rise to the bait of their challenges. You have to remain calm and objective enough not to take their comments or attitudes personally" (p. 198).

Some parents make two tactical errors in these kinds of tense situations. First, they blame themselves for their child's unacceptable behavior: *It's my fault. If only I were a better parent.* Second, they feel pressure to change that behavior on the spot in one act of parental force and discipline: *This is unacceptable. I have to power up and put a stop to such foolishness.*

When you feel the urge to blame yourself or "go nuclear"—or both—*don't do it.* Let it go. It's not your fault. Your daughter is a kid being a kid and trying to figure out how to navigate life. Accept that for your own sake and for your daughter's.

Then remember the wisdom of this old saying: "Be kind, for everyone you meet is fighting a great battle." In other words, remind yourself that the root issue is not your daughter's rolled eyes or aloofness or withering comments. Those are symptoms of a deeper issue inside. Something is bothering her, and you need to gently and wisely figure out what that is. How would you respond if she were showing signs of some sort of physical illness? You wouldn't take it personally. In fact, you would show great love and gentleness. You need to take the same approach here.

Spend a few minutes mulling over the apostle Paul's words to the ancient church at Colossae:

> Since God chose you to be the holy people he loves, you must clothe yourselves with tenderhearted mercy, kindness, humility, gentleness, and patience. Make allowance for each other's faults, and forgive anyone who offends you. Remember, the Lord forgave you, so you must forgive others. Above all, clothe yourselves with love, which binds us all together in perfect harmony. And let the peace that comes from Christ rule in your hearts. For as members of one body you are called to live in peace. And always be thankful. (Colossians 3:12–15, NLT)

Trying to like a kid who's not always likable? Paul says respond to unlikable behavior with mercy, gentleness, and patience. Make allowances. Forgive the way you have been forgiven by God and the way you need (and want) to be forgiven by others when you haven't exactly exhibited stellar character. Ask Christ, the Prince of Peace, to rule in your heart and in your home.

PRAY

God, help me with Your grace to practice mercy and patience, love and acceptance, even when I feel impatient with my daughter. Amen.

FLEX YOUR DAD MUSCLES

Your daughter has a primal need to be liked. In ways she can't even understand, much less articulate, she wants to be liked by you even if she's been acting terribly lately. So surprise her. Pick out one or two qualities you admire in your daughter, and tell her about them. Or if things are so bad that you are barely on speaking terms, write her a note and put it on her desk or her pillow.

Depending on her mood, she might toss it in the trash can or start an argument. That's okay. Wait a few days and do it again. If she tries to pick a fight, refuse to take the bait. Just continue to communicate that you genuinely like her.

I don't want to give you unrealistic expectations. The breakthrough you're looking for might take a while. I just know you can't give up and that gentle and courageous perseverance—even when you feel like saying, "Forget it!"—will eventually lead to changes. Depending on your situation, it might take days, it might take weeks, it might take months, it might even take a year, but if you follow Paul's advice and clothe yourself with "tenderhearted mercy, kindness, humility, gentleness, and patience," you will be rewarded—and your daughter will, in the goodness of time, thank you.

LISTENING

Understand this, my dear brothers and sisters: You must all be
quick to listen, slow to speak, and slow to get angry.
—James 1:19, NLT

Many of my pediatric patients have told me in so many words, "My parents never listen to me—they just lecture all the time." If we're honest, listening isn't a strength for most people. It's a great cultural weakness for a number of reasons. First of all, listening is a skill, no different than laying ceramic tile or smoking ribs. It's something we have to learn how to do. It requires training. Someone has to teach us. Somewhere in your past, you might have enrolled in a scuba diving class, signed up for a gun safety course, taken golf lessons, or attended a seminar on public speaking. But have you ever seen, much less taken, a workshop in listening?

Another reason we struggle as listeners is that listening takes time, and time is the one thing that is always in short supply. We're always rushing from thing to thing, trying to pack it all in. As long as you are in a hurry, you'll fail at listening, because it's impossible to listen in a hurry. Since the mouth usually has to speak a lot of words to express what the heart is really trying to say, listening always involves slowing down.

Listening is rare because it requires us to pay attention, which is tough because our culture has trained us to have short attention spans. Not only that, but at any given moment a hundred loud things are clamoring for our attention—those pressing issues at work, incoming bills, a beckoning hobby, that undone home improvement project, that new toy. No wonder we're tempted to try to listen while we simultaneously focus on four other things. (I think hip-hop rapper Propaganda was on to something when he said, "Multitasking is a myth. You ain't doin' anything good, just everything awful.")

Listening—for men especially—can seem passive and pointless. This is because men tend to be fixers. Why sit and talk about problems when you could fix them? This explains why many men tune out. At the first mention of a problem, fathers immediately lose focus on what's being said. Mentally, they turn their attention to what needs to be done. The minute his daughter pauses to take a breath, Dad proudly rolls out his foolproof plan. When she tears up, Dad throws up his hands in frustration.

"Listening to *my* daughter," some fathers would object, "isn't just difficult, it's impossible. She doesn't talk. She's like an extremely introverted clam. Maybe she talks to her friends, but she clearly doesn't want to talk to me." I can only tell you from my extensive interactions with girls that this isn't true. It may feel or seem true, but it isn't. Daughters desperately want to talk to their fathers. The problem is that a lot of fathers, for the reasons listed above (and others), have unknowingly discouraged their daughters from talking. No girl is going to open up to her dad if she knows it will result in (a) a glazed look and some distracted grunts; or (b) a lengthy lecture.

Here's the thing: though listening is a difficult habit to develop, at least it's not a complicated thing. You're not required to make pronouncements—you simply offer your presence. There's no pressure to give lectures, advice, or counsel—just your attention. And here's a bonus: the fathers who excel at listening when their daughters are young are the ones who get listened to by their daughters later.

Simply engage with your daughter—and forget trying to be insightful, informative, or interesting. Just be "all ears."

When you do that, it says to your daughter, "You matter. You're special. Your life has worth. I care about what's going on with you. I find you interesting."

Don't interrupt, even when she says ridiculous things (believe me, she will). Daughters, especially teenage daughters, are dramatic. If you feel yourself getting irritated, resist the urge to blurt out reprimands or corrective statements. Let her finish a thought; then ask clarifying questions. Let her talk about her feelings, and let her know that you hear not just her words but her heart.

We've all had occasions where people obviously have checked out of our conversations. It's frustrating to know that no one is listening; and disheartening that they don't care. Don't be that person for your daughter. Be the good listener.

If you develop this precious and rare skill, your daughter will come to you again and again to sort out her tangled feelings and jumbled beliefs. Lots of times you won't have to say much at all. Your presence and quiet strength alone can often help her find the answer she seeks. And because you care to listen to her, her confidence will soar. Most important, listening will forge a deep bond between you and your daughter.

PRAY

God, I admit that listening is not my strong suit. When my daughter is chattering away about trivial matters or some inconsequential drama, my mind wanders. I think, *Do we really need to spend thirty minutes belaboring a problem that could be diagnosed and solved in thirty seconds?* Lord, please give me patience, and help me cultivate this rare habit of listening. I want to be quicker (and better) at hearing not just my daughter's words but her heart. I want to become slower to speak and get frustrated. Amen.

FLEX YOUR DAD MUSCLES

As I wrote in *Strong Fathers, Strong Daughters*, "listening is tough, particularly when the words don't make sense and the ideas seem superfluous. But listen anyway. Sit down. Look her in the eye. Don't let your mind wander. And you'll be rewarded with a daughter's trust, love, and affection" (p. 57).

Do an experiment. Commit to spend ten unhurried, uninterrupted minutes with your daughter each day for the next seven days. You don't have to do anything expensive or exotic. Be creative. Pick a low-key, age-appropriate activity that will involve minimal distractions. Sit on the porch swing—just the two of you. Work a jigsaw puzzle. Take a drive (without the radio blaring). Play catch or ping-pong. Do a simple chore together—pulling weeds or raking. Walk the dog around the block.

During whatever activity you choose, ask her two questions: What was the best thing about your day? What was the worst thing about your day? (Start with the best thing because we like sharing good news—and that will help get her talking.)

Resist the urge to interrupt. And by all means, don't become critical. Just listen. As much as possible, make eye contact. Smile. If you're not driving, turn and face her. Lean in. Hug her. Pay attention to her tone, her facial expressions, her body language. Study her (like you would that trophy buck walking toward your deer stand). Give her your undivided attention. You would do all this for your most important client—why not for the person who matters far more to you?

Do this for a week, and watch what happens.

Week 39

PICKING YOUR BATTLES

Starting a quarrel is like opening a floodgate,
so stop before a dispute breaks out.
—Proverbs 17:14, NLT

Joe Louis was the world heavyweight boxing champion from 1937 until he retired in 1949—even while serving in the Army during World War II. One day while driving a military transport, the "Brown Bomber" was involved in a fender bender with another vehicle. He was at fault. The other driver exploded out of his truck, and, not realizing the identity of the man who had collided with him, proceeded to scream and curse at Louis. The champ sat calmly and quietly in the cab of his vehicle while the man vented and spewed.

After the irate truck driver had moved on, Louis's companion asked, "Joe, why did you let that guy scream at you like that? Why didn't you get out and deck him?"

"Why should I do that?" replied the champ. "When somebody insulted Caruso, did he sing an aria for him?"

Louis's controlled response is a greater reminder that strong men don't need to flex their muscles all the time. Joe Louis knew he was the best fighter in the world. He had nothing to prove. To engage in a yelling match or physical confrontation would have solved nothing. In truth, it would only have been degrading.

I think of this story when I see how some fathers embrace a combative attitude toward their daughters. They make a federal case out of every little thing. Every roll of their daughter's eyes, every cluck of her tongue, every snide comment is met with a lecture or a rebuke or a consequence.

Pretty soon, the atmosphere in such homes is so supercharged that everyone is constantly walking on pins and needles. The sense that "a fight could break out at any moment" is palpable.

This reminds me of another boxing story I once heard. The manager of a different champion fighter was asked why he passed on a match that would have been an easy victory and a huge payday for his fighter. His response was genius: "My guy only has so many fights in him. I'm not about to use up one of 'em on an opponent like that!"

What a wise word. We only have so many fights in us (at least only a few that are worth fighting). Why be belligerent? Why go to war over silly stuff? Why pick fights? This is exactly what Proverbs 20:3 warns us not to do: "It is to one's honor to avoid strife, but every fool is quick to quarrel" (NIV).

I encourage parents to choose their battles wisely—to invoke discipline only in cases of flagrant, intentional defiance and not when a kid is just being a kid.

Dr. James Dobson discusses this idea in his bestselling book *Dare to Discipline.* Let's say you have a two-year-old who turns her bowl of oatmeal upside down and smears the sticky stuff all over the table. Is she trying to be bad? No, she's just having fun. If your eleven-year-old sneaks her mom's eyeliner into her backpack and puts it on at school, is she trying to be defiant? No, she feels insecure and is probably trying to make friends and fit in. What if your seventeen-year-old daughter misses the deadline for registering for a big college entrance exam? She's probably not trying to make you mad. She's a girl living inside the body of a woman, but she doesn't have a woman's brain yet.

These are all annoying behaviors, but they come with being a kid or a teenager. They are not necessarily acts of open rebellion against you. If, however, you looked into the eyes of your two-year-old and said, "Do not dump your cereal bowl over!"; or you told your eleven-year-old daughter, "You are not allowed to wear makeup at school"; or if you told your teenage daughter, "Here's the money to register for your college entrance exam," and she spent it at the mall instead; then discipline is called for.

When kids cross a line that has been drawn in the sand, you must respond immediately and firmly. This means serious, age-appropriate consequences should follow. Maybe the two-year-old goes into a time-out for two minutes every time she dumps the bowl over. (And, get ready: a strong-willed two-year-old may spend hours dumping it over and over to see how long it takes to break your resolve.) Maybe the eleven-year-old is forbidden to go to friends' homes for a week or two. Maybe you make the seventeen-year-old pay for the next exam herself, and take away her car or phone privileges.

Winning these battles with disobedient children is crucial; this is serious business and needs to be taken seriously. You can't tell your daughter, "We're confiscating your cell phone for a week," and then, weary of her incessant complaining, give it back to her a couple of days later simply to keep her quiet.

If you give in to your children when they're young, their behavior will only get worse when they get older. The manipulation, the wheedling, the games, and the tantrums become more sophisticated and more intense. Dad, be warned: the more you give in, the harder it will be to lay down the law later. One surrender and you have given back not only her phone, you have, in her mind, surrendered your authority.

Because the stakes are high, pick your battles wisely. Ignore the little things. Embrace the spirit of 1 Peter 4:8: "Most important of all, continue to show deep love for each other, for *love covers a multitude of sins*" (emphasis added, NLT).

But on the aggressively defiant stuff, take action. Go to war on that. Stand your ground—don't let her wear you down.

PRAY

God, thank You for not taking me to task for every single mistake and boneheaded choice I make. Your grace is greater than all my sin. With my daughter I need wisdom. I want to love her well. I want the battles she and I fight to be the ones worth fighting. Give me the strength to fight those battles to the end. Amen.

FLEX YOUR DAD MUSCLES

Take some time—with your wife, if possible—to evaluate your approach to discipline. You might want to ask these questions:

- Do I have a "philosophy of discipline"?
- Where is it succeeding?
- Where is it failing?
- What battles might be looming with our daughter?
- What little things should I probably just let slide?

Week 40

PRACTICING GRATITUDE

Give thanks in all circumstances;
for this is God's will for you in Christ Jesus.
—1 Thessalonians 5:18, NIV

"**M**y daughter doesn't appreciate one thing her mother and I do for her," a frustrated Steven recently lamented. "Saturday was Kacey's sixth birthday. We went all out. Karla made this awesome cake with some Disney character on it—I can't remember which one—some girl with red hair. Anyway, it looked amazing. I went out and rented a big, inflatable bouncy thing and put it in the front yard. We invited about fifteen of her friends.

"Everyone was having a ball—except Kacey. She acted like a total brat—pouting one minute and being rude the next. I whispered to Karla, 'What is her deal?' She shrugged and said, 'Maybe she's just overwhelmed with all the attention?'

"Well, we got through the party, then later that evening, when we did our own little family celebration, we gave Kacey a few smaller gifts, then a new bicycle. It was more of the same. She actually said, 'Is this it?' And she *never* once said, 'Thanks, Mom and Dad.' Not one time.

"That night, lying in bed, the thought hit me: *It wasn't just today; Kacey never acts appreciative.* Karla and I talked and decided that's not right. That's got to change. We're not raising an ungrateful kid."

If I were wearing a hat right now, I'd tip it to Steven and Karla. We need more parents like them. We need to be teaching our children to be grateful. Our kids need to learn to appreciate all that they have. And they need to learn gratefulness from us.

In the Scripture verse cited above, the command is to be thankful in "all circumstances." This means the practice of showing gratitude isn't to be an occasional activity, but a way of life. We are to express thankfulness in *good* circumstances, *ho-hum* circumstances, and *lousy* circumstances. Here's why that's difficult.

When times are *good*, it is easy to forget God. In one sense, the whole Old Testament book of Deuteronomy is a warning to the ancient Israelites (and to us) against the common tendency to take blessings for granted or to think humans are somehow responsible for their good fortune.

Mindful of this foible in human nature, the apostle Paul asked a great question: "What do you have that God hasn't given you?" (1 Corinthians 4:7, NLT). James echoed this sentiment when he wrote, "Every good and perfect gift is from above, coming down from the Father" (James 1:17, NIV).

In *ho-hum* times, we might compare our lot in life with others and become discontented.

In *lousy* times, giving *thanks* is usually far from our minds.

But we are called to "give thanks in all circumstances." When we give gratitude to God, no matter what our circumstances, we affirm that nothing has entered our experience that God hasn't orchestrated, ordained, or permitted, and that we trust Him to eventually bring good things out of bad.

When you cultivate gratitude, it builds humility. Submitting to God's purposes stretches and strengthens your faith. It also gives you a more hopeful outlook.

All this is wonderful. But here's the added bonus: as you "give thanks in all circumstances," your daughter has a ringside seat. She gets to see firsthand the transforming power of gratitude.

Okay, some parents say, *that's all fine and good, but can my self-centered child really learn to be appreciative like that?* Absolutely.

The best time to start teaching kids is right from the start. As they mature, teach them to say thank you when they receive a birthday gift. When Grandma knits your daughter a bulky sweater for Christmas, coach her how to express appreciation (even though she may think it is hideous).

Expect this same courtesy at home. Your daughter should show gratitude for everything you and your wife do on her behalf.

One way to cultivate gratitude in your daughter is to give her regular household chores. Ask her to cook with you. Have her do the dishes. Show her how to do the laundry. Help her save her money to buy gifts for family members. If she's driving, expect her to pay a portion of her insurance (even a small amount will help her appreciate the cost). Shared work and shared chores are greater teachers. Thank her for working hard—and expect thanks in return. And maybe say a joint prayer of gratitude to God for all His many blessings.

Our goal as parents should echo what Sir John Templeton said: "How wonderful it would be if we could help our children and grandchildren to learn thanksgiving at an early age. Thanksgiving opens the doors. It changes a child's personality. A child is resentful, negative—or thankful. Thankful children want to give, they radiate happiness, they draw people."

Gratitude is a recognition of our blessings that encourages us to bless others. Make it part of your family's life.

Pray

God, I pray that I might be thankful in all circumstances today; and I pray that I might help my daughter develop a grateful and thankful heart. Amen.

Flex Your Dad Muscles

Sit down with your daughter and make lists of all the things you are grateful for—and then challenge each other to expand your lists. When you think your lists are finished, discuss this quote from Helen Keller, which helps put things in perspective: "I thank God for my handicaps, for, through them, I have found myself, my work, and my God." Take a minute to memorize with your daughter 1 Thessalonians 5:18.

Week 41

PRAYING

One day Jesus told his disciples a story to show
that they should always pray and never give up.
—Luke 18:1, NLT

Kids are innately curious about God.

I say this all the time—not to be provocative or preachy, but because it's true. This is why a small child (even from an irreligious home) will naturally ask questions like, "What color is God? Could God jump over the moon?" Regardless of how uncomfortable you may be with discussions about faith, or how inadequate you might feel talking about such matters, your child wants help and guidance from you in this area.

Here's another truth: the first exposure your children will have to issues of faith and spirituality is through you. In every important matter, kids look first to Mom or Dad for answers. If they don't come right out and ask, at the very least they watch closely for hints and clues. You might find this intimidating, but it should be encouraging. It means you have the power to influence your daughter's spirituality in a profound way.

Kids often see God as a heavenly version of their own father. So your example will determine whether she initially thinks of God as kind and understanding or explosive, irritable, and hard to please.

The other way you immediately shape your daughter's view of God is through prayer. Prayer is *faith in action*, and your daughter should see you in prayer often.

You should pray *for* your daughter, of course, but you should also pray *with* her. Make it a daily ritual, at night, in the morning, before meals.

Teach her that prayer is a way of conversing with God, a way to thank Him for His blessings. Don't worry too much about the words. As the great John Bunyan (author of *The Pilgrim's Progress*) wrote, "In prayer, it is better to have heart without words, than words without heart."

Let your daughter know that she can turn to God anytime and anywhere throughout the day. She can bring Him anything at all—her joys, fears, needs, and questions—and He will hear her. She is never alone. God, Who loves and cares for her, is always standing by; and as Proverbs 15:8 has it: "The prayer of the upright is His delight" (NASB). God doesn't merely tolerate our prayers—He delights in the humble petitions of His children. He welcomes our pleas.

Granted not all our prayers are answered—or at least not answered on our timeline or according to our wish list. God has His own plan for us. But you can celebrate with your daughter when prayers are answered and discuss what God's plan might be when they are not. Praying with your daughter can be a very effective way for both of you to grow in faith.

So pray. Pray big bold prayers with your daughter. Ask God to work powerfully in her heart. And trust Him.

Here's how the apostle Paul (and his team of missionaries) prayed for the Christians in the ancient city of Colossae:

> . . . we have not stopped praying for you since we first heard about you. We ask God to give you complete knowledge of his will and to give you spiritual wisdom and understanding. Then the way you live will always honor and please the Lord, and

your lives will produce every kind of good fruit. All the while, you will grow as you learn to know God better and better.

We also pray that you will be strengthened with all his glorious power so you will have all the endurance and patience you need. May you be filled with joy, always thanking the Father. He has enabled you to share in the inheritance that belongs to his people, who live in the light. (Colossians 1:9–12, NLT)

By practicing prayer, you and your daughter will find yourselves closer to each other and closer to God. And believe me, no father prays like the father of a teenage girl.

PRAY

Lord, I want to be faithful in trusting You, turning to You, and depending on You. Help me to get into the habit of praying every day. I want my daughter to see that example and follow it. Amen.

FLEX YOUR DAD MUSCLES

Here are a few ways to jumpstart a life of prayer:

- Make family prayers—such as before meals—a daily ritual.

- Pray with your wife, especially about your children.
- If your daughter is young, teach her "fill-in-the-blank" prayers, such as *God, I thank You for* _____. Or *God, forgive me for* _____. Or *God, help me* _____.
- Read an informative book on prayer like *Too Busy Not to Pray: Slowing Down to Be with God* by Bill Hybels or *Prayer: Experiencing Awe and Intimacy with God* by Timothy Keller.
- Join a men's prayer group and become a "prayer warrior."

Week 42

PROBLEM SOLVING

Who can find a virtuous and capable wife? She is more precious than rubies. Her husband can trust her, and she will greatly enrich his life.... She goes to inspect a field and buys it; with her earnings she plants a vineyard. She is energetic and strong, a hard worker. She makes sure her dealings are profitable; her lamp burns late into the night. Her hands are busy spinning thread, her fingers twisting fiber. She extends a helping hand to the poor and opens her arms to the needy. She has no fear of winter for her household, for everyone has warm clothes.
—Proverbs 31:10–11, 16–21, NLT

Wouldn't you love to meet this woman? So capable. So strong. So industrious and productive. (And the excerpt above is only a small portion of King Lemuel's lavish praise of this woman's character and abilities.) No wonder women aspire to become—and single men hope to find—a "Proverbs 31" woman. My conclusion? She had great parents—parents who taught her, among other things, how to solve problems.

I have a girlfriend who insists there are two types of women: pioneer women and princesses. By "princesses" she means spoiled, pampered girls who always think they deserve a better life and who expect everyone else to cater to them. Such girls (or women) are "high-maintenance." They are self-centered and tend to be needy and helpless. They see themselves as victims, and they are always expecting someone to rescue them.

By "pioneer women," my friend means confident young women who have been taught to work hard and serve others. They're tough. They don't come unglued at every minor trial. They're resourceful. They're good, clear thinkers. They're marked by a healthy can-do spirit of self-reliance.

Men are natural problem solvers, and most "pioneer women" were taught by strong fathers.

In *Strong Fathers, Strong Daughters* (pp. 123–27), I tell the story of Kelly, a precocious and hyperactive kid. She came from a good home, but her conscientious, engaged parents were worn out by Kelly's unending energy. At their wits' end, they came to see me. The visit was classic. Kelly's mom wanted emotional support and to discuss how hard it was being the mother of a child with ADHD. Kelly's dad just wanted to find a solution.

Men are wired this way. As a general rule, males approach problems differently than females do. I'm stereotyping a bit, I know, but women are more inclined to want to understand and empathize. Men are less interested in discussing *how* a problem makes everyone feel; they simply want to *do* something to fix the mess. This is one of the many reasons why men and women tend to clash. But it is also why a mother and a father make a great team: they bring complementary strengths to the table. Blessed is the child who has parents who understand this.

From their fathers, daughters learn how to apply practical solutions. You fix the broken swing. You track down the missing gerbil. You do all the things that good dads do.

But that's only the start. Smart dads don't just solve problems for their little girls. They teach them to be problem solvers. This is how a father rears a pioneer woman instead of a princess.

The older your daughter gets, the more she needs to know "Here's how" instead of simply "Here you go."

It's always easier and less time-consuming to fix problems yourself, but your daughter needs to learn. Whether it's settling an argument with her brother or putting the heel back on a broken shoe, after a while, you need to let her work it out. She needs to tap into her own resources, her own creativity; she needs to know she can.

If you want your daughter to become a smart, competent woman who responds calmly and confidently to life's trials, you need to let her meet challenges as she grows up.

So prepare her for that. Show her how to do things, and then let her do it. Show her to approach a problem and then let her come up with and implement the solution.

Being a father with a daughter is a partnership—not just with your wife, but with the future adult you're raising.

You're a strong father; work now to make sure she's a strong daughter.

PRAY

God, so many times I'd rather just swoop in and fix my daughter's problems and be done with them. But I know this isn't good for my daughter in the long run. Give me creativity and wisdom to see new ways to use problems to teach my daughter problem-solving skills. I don't want to raise a princess. I want to raise a Proverbs 31 pioneer woman. Help me take some steps to do this today. Amen.

FLEX YOUR DAD MUSCLES

One way to get your daughter thinking about problem solving is to play the scenario game. Ask her what she would do if:

- She forgot her lunch at home.
- Her bike chain fell off.
- She woke up and didn't have a clean outfit for school.
- A friend suggested they watch an inappropriate movie.
- She had a big test coming up in a difficult class.
- Her friend refused to return a sweater she borrowed.

Another way to learn problem solving is to pass on some basic skills:

- How to change a flat tire (on her bike or the car).
- How to use the washer and dryer.
- How to fry the perfect egg (or grill the perfect burger).
- How to back up her work on the computer.
- How to replace the toner cartridge in the printer.
- How to iron a shirt.
- How to start the lawn mower.
- How to use jumper cables.
- How to tie a few basic knots.
- How to hammer a nail.
- Ten amazing uses of duct tape.
- What to do after a fender bender.

PROTECTING

Even when I walk through the darkest valley,
I will not be afraid, for you are close beside me.
Your rod and your staff protect and comfort me.
—Psalms 23:4, NLT

eing a parent is like living with your heart outside your chest. Watching your baby walk into school for the first time or wobble down the sidewalk on a bike with no training wheels, you feel raw and vulnerable. That first time your daughter sleeps over at a friend's house, drives off by herself after getting her license, or goes to a big dance, all your protective instincts are on high alert.

Trust me. As a mother and a grandmother, I know that "mama-bear-protecting-its-cubs" feeling. I also know that for you, being the daddy of a little girl (or a teenage daughter) awakens emotions and impulses that you never even knew you had. It's weird, isn't it? That teenage daughter who, just a few years ago as a little girl, was terrified of the dark, now is asking you if she can stay out all night.

I don't have to tell you that your paternal fears and protective instincts are well-founded. You see all the distressing stories on your Facebook feed. You hear anecdotes from friends. As a pediatrician for more than three decades, I have seen firsthand the terrible things that can happen to our kids. So what's a father to do?

I think it's worth considering that in a real sense a father is a shepherd, and his family is his flock. The Bible uses such pastoral imagery frequently. Look again at the verse above. It's a line from perhaps the most famous chapter of the Bible—Psalm 23.

In that prayer-song, David likens himself to a sheep, and he pictures God—His heavenly Father—as a shepherd. Notice what David says. Essentially, as he encounters scary situations, he does so without fear. Why? Because God is with him and God protects him.

That's a great image or snapshot of God's character. It's also a great reminder of how earthly dads should care for their little (or big) girls. Be present. Be engaged. Be *with* them so you can watch over them and so you can protect them from scary things. Here are four specific ways a strong father needs to guard his daughter:

Protect her mentally. In *Strong Fathers, Strong Daughters*, I tell the story of Anna, a fourth-grader, who suddenly (and inexplicably) became antagonistic toward her dad. It took months of probing to trace her mood change to its roots. Unsupervised, Anna had witnessed a graphic sex scene (possibly a rape) while flipping channels. This had traumatized Anna, and she projected this kind of hurtful behavior onto her father. Thankfully, we were finally able to talk about this incident; otherwise Anna might have harbored distorted views about sex and men (including her own father) for years.

You cannot be too careful. With the Internet, a child is only a mouse click or two away from real dangers. Predators lure kids in on YouTube via "harmless videos." Adult content is also easily available on popular social media apps like Twitter, Pinterest, and Tumblr. This is why I always counsel fathers: do *not* let a child have a TV or a computer in their bedroom. Restrict Internet usage and TV time to when you or your wife can supervise. (By the way, if your daughter sees you looking at things you tell her not to look at, it sends a really bad and confusing signal.)

Some dads feel the need to resort to even more drastic measures. They pull the plug on their TV altogether. Or they use parental controls and block certain channels. Many have Internet filters.

Unless you go live in the wilderness "off the grid" or refuse to let her out of the house until she's grown, you cannot keep your daughter from exposure to everything. You can, however, limit the things that come into her mind. You are a shepherd to your daughter. It's your responsibility to guard her (as much as possible).

Protect her physically and sexually. I have written extensively on these matters in my books *Your Kids at Risk: How Teen Sex Threatens Our Sons and Daughters* and *Strong Fathers, Strong Daughters*. The subtitle to *Your Kids at Risk* summarizes what the research shows: teen sex is killing our kids. Currently, one in four teenagers is living with one of more than thirty sexually transmitted infections. Consequently, depression among teenage girls and boys is off the charts. How can you keep your daughter from such heartache? In short, connect with her. Talk with her. Hug her. (Girls who receive lots of appropriate physical affection from their fathers are less likely to seek out inappropriate sexual attention.) You be the judge of what she wears and don't let her go to un-chaperoned parties. You have to be courageous enough to be "the bad guy"—or she will end up in the arms of a truly bad guy.

Protect her socially. Get to know your daughter's school friends and their parents. This takes effort, but it is the best way to know who is influencing your child. Attend parent-teacher conferences. Ask about any educational concerns to be sure, but also ask about your daughter's social interactions and about any concerns regarding bullying. Away from school, let your house become the hangout. Encourage your daughter to have her friends come over. Without hovering, ask them questions about themselves (kids love talking about themselves). What do they like and dislike? What's their sibling situation? Where do they live? In this way you will learn not just about the kids themselves but also about their home life, what their parents are like, if both work, if mom and dad are separated or divorced. You *don't* want to turn this into an inquisition, but you *do* want to be curious and interested. The point is not to be judgmental; it is to protect your daughter.

If your daughter gets an invite to visit a friend, call the parents and get details. If after asking your questions, your gut tells you something is "off," follow your instincts.

Protect her spiritually. I routinely tell parents that kids do better in life when they have faith, a genuine belief in God. I say this unashamedly because (a) I've seen the research; and (b) I've talked to thousands of children and teenagers. Protecting your daughter spiritually can mean a lot of things. Mostly it means providing her with answers to her questions. Remember, she doesn't want sermons; she does, however, want to know what you think. The more you grow in your faith, the more you can help her. This is important because there are some religious groups and movements (even cults) that advocate some wacky ideas. Your daughter needs your help in order to see that not every so-called truth is true.

I'm not trying to sensationalize the ills that confront your daughter. I'm trying to inform you so that you can act out of strength, not fear. Don't fade into the background of your daughter's life. Be a shepherd. Pick up your "rod and your staff" and protect her. If you don't, who will?

PRAY

Father in heaven, thanks for shepherding me and protecting me. I want to do the same for my daughter. Make me aware of specific threats. Give me the wisdom and the courage to do what needs to be done. Amen.

FLEX YOUR DAD MUSCLES

If your daughter is eleven or older, have a conversation where you let her know that: (1) you are on her side, and she can come to you at any time with any problem (even if she feels embarrassed); (2) lots of the things that many of her friends will start doing when they turn twelve, thirteen, or fourteen are really harmful (things like watching certain movies or experimenting with sex, alcohol, and drugs).

Explain that because of this, you want to talk about screen time. This includes anything she views on the computer, video games she plays, songs she listens to, and movies and TV shows she watches. Bring up a movie she recently saw. Ask, "What did you like? What did you dislike?" (Hint: When you ask good questions, you can lead your children to good conclusions, and they will listen because they feel like they came up with the answers.) Pay attention. If your daughter says, "Uh, I don't know, I guess it was kind of violent," pause and then ask something like, "Did that violence bother you?" Again, this will get her thinking.

As the conversation moves forward, ask questions like, "I know that in that sitcom there is some sex and language. Does that bother you?" Probably, your daughter will become defensive because she knows that if she says yes you'll make her stop watching, so insist you just want her opinion. Bring the conversation to a place where your daughter talks about how she really feels. Let her know that she's the target for all of this, not you. Marketers and producers want her to buy more and more of their stuff. Ask her how she feels about being manipulated and used in this way.

Tell her you want such conversations to continue, not so that you can spy on her, but so that you can help her see her way clearly in a world that wants to shape her values and thoughts. Tell her you don't want her to be a victim of wrong ideas. You won't be able to cover everything in one talk, but this is a terrific beginning to what can be a very important ongoing conversation.

SERVING

You, my brothers and sisters, were called to be free.
But do not use your freedom to indulge the flesh;
rather, serve one another humbly in love.
—Galatians 5:13, NIV

O ne night when our kids were little, my husband and I made a deal: I would order Chinese takeout for dinner (a family favorite) if he would go pick up our order. He happily agreed.

Just before he left the house, I reminded him, "Make sure they don't forget to include the egg rolls!" (*my* personal favorite part of the meal). He nodded, two of our daughters jumped in the car with him, and off they went.

When they returned home, we put all the food out on the table. There were lots of little white boxes—but not a single egg roll! I voiced my bewilderment (translation: I barked at my husband in great frustration): "I told you *as you were walking out the door,* 'Don't forget the egg rolls!'"

My husband hung his head. In the uncomfortable silence that followed, my six-year-old tugged on my sleeve and whispered in my ear that on the way home from the restaurant, her daddy had spotted a man rummaging through some garbage cans. He immediately pulled over into the parking lot nearby, called out to the man, and explained that he had several bags of Chinese food. "Sir, you are welcome to any or all of this," my husband offered. You guessed it. The man took my beloved egg rolls.

Our daughters have never forgotten that incident—even though it happened years and years ago. Those few moments in a dark parking lot gave them a vivid picture of what it looks like to treat others as you would like to be treated. That one simple act imprinted the idea of charity on my daughters' hearts much more powerfully than a hundred sermons or Sunday school lessons. They got to see up close their father live out one of the great themes of the Bible—serving others.

Listen to the words God spoke to His people through the prophet Isaiah: "What I'm interested in seeing you do is: sharing your food with the hungry, inviting the homeless poor into your homes, putting clothes on the shivering ill-clad, being available to your own families" (Isaiah 58:6–7, MSG).

Notice the way Jesus described the purpose of His life: "For even the Son of Man did not come to be served, but to serve, and to give His life a ransom for many" (Mark 10:45, NASB).

Consider how the apostle Paul called all God's people to live: "In your relationships with one another, have the same mindset as Christ Jesus: Who, being in very nature God, did not consider equality with God something to be used to his own advantage; rather, he made himself nothing by taking the very nature of a servant" (Philippians 2:5–7, NIV).

The point is, you don't have to dig deep into the Scriptures to see that serving others is considered a necessary, even mandatory, aspect of the spiritual life. Serving is Faith 101. Yet we serve, less out of obligation, and more out of a sense of awe and gratitude. Servant-minded people are humbled at how God has blessed them. Knowing they are eternally secure in His grace and stunned that He would want to use them to enrich the lives of others, they feel both compelled and eager to serve. When you have been bowled over by God's kindness to you, "not serving" is not an option. It's a very natural (or, more accurately, a supernatural) response.

Martin Luther King Jr. said, "Life's most persistent and urgent question is, 'What are you doing for others?'" On another occasion he said, "Everybody can be great, because anybody can serve. You don't have to have a college degree to serve. You don't have to make your subject and verb agree to serve. You only need a heart full of grace, a soul generated by love."

How can we serve others?

Look. Pastor Adele Calhoun says that "Service is rooted in *seeing*." And she encourages us to see others as God does: "God cares about productive and nonproductive people, poor people and rich people, educated and noneducated people. God cares about everybody."

Help. If you're not normally helpful around the house, make a change. Start helping with the dishes. Offer to do the laundry. Or, outside your home, get involved in a soup kitchen or a food drive.

Invite. Don't serve all by yourself. Make service a family affair. Have your daughter serve side-by-side with you. It will be a great life lesson.

In a world that tells your daughter to think, *It's all about ME*, show her a radically different way to live. Let her experience the truth of what Pierre Teilhard de Chardin said: "The most satisfying thing in life is to have been able to give a large part of one's self to others."

Point. In your serving, always point your daughter back to God. (In truth, there's no way to teach your daughter about God without talking about service; God served us by sending Christ. And Christ honored God through a whole-life commitment to service.) John Henry Newman said it well: "God has created me to do Him some definite service; He has committed some work to me which He has not committed to another.... I have a part in this great work; I am a link in a chain, a bond of connection between persons. He has not created me for naught. I shall do good, I shall do His work."

If your daughter leaves home without a clear sense that she is loved unconditionally by God, and should treat others as fellow children of God, serving them with dignity and respect, she is in for a miserable life.

She needs to learn humility, and the best way to cultivate this essential virtue is to serve God by serving others. As the apostle Paul admonished,

"Serve wholeheartedly, as if you were serving the Lord, not people" (Ephesians 6:7, NIV).

I can tell you from experience, there's nothing like the joy and satisfaction of serving others—even when it costs you your beloved egg rolls.

PRAY

God, help me commit myself to a life of service, so that in everything I do—at work, at home, in volunteer projects—I might offer greater glory to You and teach my daughter the virtue of service. Amen.

FLEX YOUR DAD MUSCLES

Read and discuss the story of the Good Samaritan (Luke 10:25–37) with your daughter, and then ask:

- How can we help more around the house?
- How can we better serve people in our neighborhood?
- How can we better serve our community?

When you've got some ideas, put them in action.

Week 45

SETTING BOUNDARIES

*Am I now trying to win the approval of human beings, or of
God? Or am I trying to please people? If I were still trying to
please people, I would not be a servant of Christ.*
—Galatians 1:10, NIV

T hings are complicated right now at the Benson household. Let's
take a peek:

Stan just took off on a rare evening jog, hoping to burn off
some serious frustration. What's got him so worked up? When he picked
up his thirteen-year-old daughter from tennis team practice, her coach
broke the news that Charissa would no longer be playing as the team's
third seed. "I need to drop her down to six, Stan. She's not progressing. If
anything, she's regressing. I'm sorry. Hope you understand." This news
precipitated a heated daddy-daughter discussion on the way home. It began
with Stan accusing Charissa of not doing her best. It ended with her sobbing uncontrollably.

Then, right as Stan walked in the back door, his mother phoned.
Within ten minutes she had gotten her reluctant son to agree to come over
on the weekend. "It's a cookout for some ex-neighbors who are passing
through town," Stan ranted to his wife, Ellen. "People I haven't seen—I
haven't even *thought about*—in at least twenty years. Why in the world

did I agree to give up my entire Saturday afternoon and evening, when I really need to be painting the guest room?"

Everything in Ellen wanted to say, "Because your mom is manipulative and you can't tell her no." But she wisely bit her tongue—even as she begrudgingly started another colossal load of laundry, 90 percent of which was from Charissa's room (because even if their fashion-obsessed daughter merely tries on an article of clothing, it goes in the dirty clothes hamper).

Meanwhile, upstairs Charissa is texting with a friend about how much she hates tennis: "Id quit tmrw if my dad wudnt freak out."

Sounds to me like the Bensons need some *boundaries* that establish my life from yours. For instance, in the Benson house Stan needs to quit pushing his daughter to excel in a sport that, frankly, she's just not passionate about. Whether she plays a sport is better her call than his.

He needs to tell his mom, "Sorry, that's not going to work for me. I have other plans. Maybe next time. You guys have a blast."

Ellen needs to tell Charissa, "Sweetie, I'm not washing clothes that you wore for thirty seconds. Since you insist on going through four or five outfits a day, it's time you learned to do your own laundry."

Charissa needs to be honest with her dad and say, "I'll finish out this season, but I don't want to play tennis next year. I feel like that's *your* dream for my life, not mine."

Setting boundaries with friends or family isn't easy. It can seem counterintuitive. *Of course as a father I should push my daughter in sports, because she'll appreciate it later,* or *Of course I should say yes to the invitation—she's my mother after all.* We don't want to appear mean or selfish, we don't want to seem like we're not doing our part. But I promise you that setting boundaries is necessary for healthy relationships and fulfilling lives; and your daughter, as always, needs to learn from your example. Here's how to start.

Seek God. Pray. God wants you to live out *His* calling, not be enslaved to someone else's agenda for your life. If you're feeling overstretched, remember what the apostle Peter says, "Give all your worries and cares to God, for he cares about you" (1 Peter 5:7, NLT). Prayer can help you find a saner, healthier way to live.

Simplify. Look at your schedule. Are you doing too much? Do you even *like* all the things you're doing? Is there an unnecessary, undesirable activity you could eliminate from your schedule this week?

Say no. We can't always be in motion, always working or attending events or helping out. A spiritual life, a life of prayer, requires some downtime, some solitude. You need to take it—and not feel guilty about it.

Skin in the game. When your daughter breaks her cell phone for the umpteenth time and turns to you to buy a replacement, tell her that the buck stops with her. If she wants a new phone, she has to pay for it. Giving everyone in the family some "skin in the game" is another good way of setting boundaries and establishing a sense of personal responsibility.

Show and tell. Help your daughter set boundaries that will protect her, including:

- *Physical boundaries.* When she's little, remind her she is in charge of her body—that no one should touch or see under her swimsuit areas except her mom or dad or her doctor. Let her know that no one should hit her. Teach her that she must also respect others in the same way. (For a more in-depth discussion of how to have such "boundary conversations," check out The Strong Parent Project online program.)
- *Emotional boundaries.* Your daughter must learn she is responsible for *her* behavior, speech, feelings, and actions. She is *not* responsible for the behavior, feelings, or speech of anyone else (including you, her mother, friends, or siblings). This is a tough lesson for kids to grasp because they are fundamentally

egocentric, at least until their early twenties, and think they can change the world, including everyone in it. You have to teach her that she is responsible for her own life, currently accountable to you, and ultimately to God.

You will also need to teach her to be assertive. I encourage you to ask your daughter not only *what* she did at school but how she *felt* about events that happened during her day. This helps her develop what I call an "emotional vocabulary." By talking in this way, kids gradually learn how to express themselves and how to own their feelings. This kind of assertiveness is essential to set healthy boundaries—and prevent others from setting them for her.

- *Social boundaries.* Every girl wants to fit in. And every dad wants his daughter to be accepted and not be relegated to the fringes. And yet, if we encourage our kids to dress just like their friends and engage in all the same activities, we're not teaching them to be independent. That's not how they learn to set healthy social boundaries.

  Step up to the plate, Dad. Especially in the area of social media. The very premise of social media is inherently contrary to boundary-setting. The point of social media is to give friends (and even acquaintances and strangers) a window into the intimate parts of one's life. This is why social media hurts so many. Kids (adults too) post way too much information and open themselves up for pain. Set limits on what she can post, monitor her social media activities, and take away her social media privileges if she abuses them.

- *Practical boundaries.* Teach her how to manage her time—from waking up in the morning to doing her homework at night—and show her how to be responsible for her clothes, her toys, her room, her electronic devices.

Strong dads help their daughters set strong boundaries.

PRAY

God, help me to live for You and to follow the calling You have set for me, and help me to show my daughter how to find her own path in life, the path You have established for her. Amen.

FLEX YOUR DAD MUSCLES

Ask yourself: Have I set all the appropriate boundaries I should have for my daughter? If you've neglected something, resolve to fix that.

And then ask: Have I set appropriate boundaries for myself? Am I trying to assert too much control? Am I too willing to say yes to things I don't want to do?

If there's an invitation you want to decline, an activity that does nothing for your family and is not part of your calling…be a leader and just say, no.

Week 46

SHOWING AFFECTION

Moved with compassion, Jesus touched their eyes;
and immediately they regained their sight and followed Him.
—Matthew 20:34, NASB

As a doctor, I can give you reams of data on how physical touch and affection can have a dramatic effect on your daughter's life. But have you ever noticed how often the gospels tell us about Jesus touching or embracing someone:

- *When a leper asked if Jesus might be willing to heal him*: "Moved with compassion, Jesus stretched out His hand and touched him, and said to him, 'I am willing; be cleansed'" (Mark 1:41, NASB).
- *When the disciples were terrified and hugging the ground after seeing the glory of God*: "Then Jesus came over and touched them. 'Get up,' he said. 'Don't be afraid'" (Matthew 17:7, NLT).
- *When parents understood Jesus' great love and affection for children*: "One day some parents brought their children to Jesus so he could touch and bless them" (Mark 10:13, NLT).

- *When Jesus arrived in a village in which many people were sick*: "As the sun went down that evening, people throughout the village brought sick family members to Jesus. No matter what their diseases were, the touch of his hand healed every one" (Luke 4:40, NLT).
- *When Jesus encountered a woman who had been crippled for eighteen years and could not stand straight*: "When Jesus saw her, he called her over and said, 'Dear woman, you are healed of your sickness!' Then he touched her, and instantly she could stand straight. How she praised God!" (Luke 13:12–13, NLT).
- *When Jesus arrived at a home where He'd been summoned to heal a sick girl, but found her already passed away*: "After the crowd had been put outside, he went in and took the girl by the hand, and she got up" (Matthew 9:25, NIV).

Clearly, the mere presence of Christ was powerful. His words were life changing. But something about His gentle and loving *touch* brought great healing and wholeness, hope and life.

And it is true that even on a human, rather than a godly, scale, the way we show physical affection for each other can have a powerful impact on our health and well-being.

Some dads roll their eyes when they hear me talk about why they need to show physical affection for their daughters. Often this is because when they try to hug their own adolescent daughters they get looks of disdain, reluctant shudders, and stiffened shoulders.

But there is a reason our daughter reacts that way—and it has nothing to do with you or her not wanting or needing your physical affection. Most preteens and adolescents are already extremely uncomfortable with their bodies and with their sexuality. A hug from mom or a kiss from dad just makes them feel that much more awkward.

Yet our kids need and want physical affection. If you go to a football or basketball game at your local high school and watch teenagers, you'll see all kinds of physical contact. And very little of it is sexual in nature. Boys will high-five and fist-bump each other. They will bear-hug each other from behind, lift each other in the air, and engage in mini wrestling matches. Girls will braid each other's hair and hug each other like long-lost friends (about every five minutes or so). What these kids are looking for is *intimacy*, which, in this context, has nothing to do with sex but everything to do with building a close personal connection.

Physical touch lets teenagers know that someone notices them and likes them. So when a dad—still the most important person in a girl's life—gives his daughter an affectionate squeeze or a tender kiss on the forehead, it affects her deeply. In fact, through hugs and forehead kisses, a girl is reaffirmed in her sense of being loved, and it helps her learn self-respect and appropriate physical modesty. Pondering the importance and power of touch, I always think of the legacy of Mother Teresa. She walked the filthy streets of Calcutta. When she found a person dying, apparently forgotten, she would take the victim's face in her hands, look directly into his eyes, and let him know that someone cared and recognized his human dignity. Through such simple touches of love, Mother Teresa communicated compassion and respect. She did this without expecting anything in return.

This is the kind of unconditional love fathers need to be offering their daughters. Determine, with God's help, to be a dad who shows affection through physical touch.

PRAY

God, help me use the power of physical touch to bless and encourage my daughter, to remind her of her self-worth, to teach her modesty, and to keep her from all harm. Amen.

FLEX YOUR DAD MUSCLES

Perhaps you're saying, "Okay, all that may be true, but it doesn't change the fact that my daughter recoils when I try to give her a hug."

If that's true, start by sitting next to her on the couch. Or, as she passes you in the kitchen, pat her on the back, or come up beside her and give her a quick side hug. If you hold hands at the dinner table when you say grace, give her hand a gentle squeeze when you say "Amen." Repeat these little gestures often. Be respectful and understand that for some girls—especially as they move through puberty—it's a process to learn how to accept touch. Just know that touches and hugs are very important. In order for your daughter to develop a healthy view of sexuality and physical expression, she needs to learn from you what it means to be handled gently and respectfully.

Needless to say (but I'll say it anyway), never allow anyone to touch your child in an inappropriate way. This will confuse her deeply and cause her to shun even healthy expressions of physical intimacy. If you ever suspect that someone (inside or outside your family) has touched your daughter in a sexual way, deal with the situation immediately.

SOUL CARE

Guard your heart above all else,
for it determines the course of your life.
—Proverbs 4:23, NLT

I f you met Randy, you'd like him immediately. In fact, if you had a ten-minute conversation with him, you'd want him for a friend and a next-door neighbor. He's outgoing, personable, and laugh-out-loud funny.

Randy is, by all accounts, a devoted husband to Connie, his high school sweetheart, and a great dad to his nine-year-old daughter and six-year-old son. He owns a successful insurance business. He coaches girls' softball. He's in a hunting club with some old college buddies, and he's active in a men's group at his church.

To most folks, it seems like Randy's life is picture-perfect. But over the last few weeks, some tiny cracks have begun to mar the image. For example,

- Randy's been unusually "short" with his kids, snapping angrily at them over every little thing.
- He's resumed an old bad habit of viewing images on his computer that he shouldn't.

- He's begun making excuses to skip his men's group (he's only been to two of the last five meetings—and the thing is, he genuinely likes these guys).
- He's become extremely anxious about finances (especially as Connie talks more and more about wanting to build a new house in a posh new neighborhood northeast of town).
- Perhaps because of that nervousness, he's put on about ten pounds of weight.

This morning was the final straw. On his way to work, a delivery truck abruptly pulled out in front of him. Randy lost it. He snapped. In his rage, he let fly a string of expletives he hasn't used in a long time.

His reaction was so extreme, so out of left field, and so unsettling, Randy sat in his car for a good ten minutes after arriving at the office. *Where did that come from? What is wrong with me?* he wondered.

Someone has said that powerful emotions are like warning lights on the dashboard of a person's life. An incident like Randy's is the soul's way of saying, "Pull over. Look under the hood. It's time to check out what's in your heart."

There's an eye-opening story in the Gospel of Matthew in which Jesus confronted the Jewish religious leaders of His day. He called them hypocrites for being obsessed with their public image when they should have been focusing on what was in their hearts. Afterward, He explained to His followers, "For from the heart come evil thoughts, murder, adultery, all sexual immorality, theft, lying, and slander" (Matthew 15:19, NLT).

This is the same idea in Solomon's proverb cited at the beginning of this chapter. Everything hinges on our hearts. If our hearts are right, our lives will be too. If our hearts aren't right—look out.

In Western culture we tend to differentiate between the head and the heart. We often say things like, "Use your head"—meaning, "Be rational;

be reasonable." Or we say, "That's your heart talking"—meaning, "You're being emotional and irrational; you're not thinking straight." In other words, we see the heart as all touchy and feely and the head or mind as all logic and facts.

But in the Bible this distinction isn't found. In Scripture the word *heart* is comprehensive. The heart is the control center of a person's life. It's where we feel, yes, but it's also where we think and reason, remember and fantasize, desire and choose. No wonder our hearts need special attention. As our hearts go, so we go. This idea is conveyed powerfully in Proverbs 4:23: "your heart…determines the course of your life."

If that's true, then we should watch over our hearts. But what does it mean, really? The Hebrew verb used for *guard* in Proverbs 4:23 is used elsewhere in the Old Testament to speak of someone who guards a vineyard or a city wall or one who tends to a fig tree. In other words, it's the idea of keeping a close eye on something, vigilantly protecting, monitoring, and caring for something. In this case, wise King Solomon tells his son to be a dedicated observer and caretaker of his own heart.

Such scrutiny of one's heart is paramount. It should be our top priority. Why? Because if our hearts aren't healthy, nothing else about our lives will be either. Our words, choices, and habits are a direct reflection of what's going on in our innermost being.

Practically speaking, what can a man like Randy do if he senses his interior life is shaky? What does it look like to have a healthy heart? Here are three quick practices for shoring up a shaky heart, or maintaining a healthy soul:

Solitude and silence. When we get off by ourselves and sit in silence we come face to face with who we really are. It's also there that we have the best chance to connect with spiritual realities. This is why God tells us in His Word, "Be still, and know that I am God" (Psalms 46:10, ESV).

Being quiet and still is a terrifying thought to many people. As Dietrich Bonhoeffer once said, "We are so afraid of silence that we chase ourselves from one event to the next in order not to have to spend a moment alone with ourselves, in order not to have to look at ourselves in the mirror." So long as we stay busy and distracted with work and extracurricular activities, so long as we immerse ourselves in noise, we cannot gauge the true conditions of our hearts. Nor will we encounter the One who can mend our disordered hearts.

Spiritual reading. Many people have seen changes within (and eventually without) through slowly and thoughtfully reading classic works of spirituality such as *The Imitation of Christ* by Thomas à Kempis, the *Pensées* of Blaise Pascal, or *My Utmost for His Highest* by Oswald Chambers. These writers were masters of the contemplative life. They offer profound insights into the intricacies of the human heart and soul.

Keeping a journal. Keeping a journal is a way for us to reflect on our actions and on God's activity in our lives. Putting your thoughts and fears on paper can have a powerful effect. Perhaps it's a version of the old Flannery O'Connor quip: "I write because I don't know what I think until I read what I say."

Strong fathers work hard to live the values they want to teach. You can't lead others effectively—or without being a hypocrite—unless you first take care of your own soul.

PRAY

God, help me to have a strong and faithful heart so that I might better lead my family. Amen.

FLEX YOUR DAD MUSCLES

Memorize Proverbs 4:23, and make it a great daily reminder.

Buy an inexpensive journal. There are no "rules" for what to write. Quotes from Scripture, prayer requests, reflections on the day, anything is fair game if it helps you maintain a healthy heart, a healthy soul.

Week 48

SPEAKING WORDS OF LIFE

Gracious words are a honeycomb,
sweet to the soul and healing to the bones.
—King Solomon, in Proverbs 16:24, NIV

I've talked often of the September evening in 1979 when a single sentence changed my life.

As a recent college graduate, I found myself living at my parents' home, discouraged, and utterly clueless about my future. The medical schools I wanted most to attend didn't want me.

That night, I passed my father's study. He was talking to a friend on the telephone. I overheard him saying, "I'm excited to tell you my daughter, Meg, will be starting medical school soon."

It was just one sentence. But those few words were life-giving. Even though in reality my father had no idea where—or *if*—I would be attending medical school, he had unwavering belief that I would go. His words of confidence infused me with confidence and a sense that I could do anything I put my mind to. In truth, they changed my life.

Ironically, years later when I reminded my father of this incident, he didn't even remember the phone call.

Fathers, your words have more power than you know.

The apostle Paul knew the power of words. He said our words should "give grace to those who hear" (Ephesians 4:29, ESV). It's a remarkable idea: we can actually speak grace into the lives of those we love. Think of the power and promise of grace. Grace lifts us when we're as low as we can be. Grace gives us hope when everything seems hopeless. Grace heals and animates us when we're lifeless and empty. The right words can do all that and more.

I know this because my father's gracious words had that kind of powerful impact on me. Over those next uncertain months, they carried and sustained me until, sure enough, in the fall of 1980, I began medical school.

Solomon compared such words to a honeycomb. The idea is they are refreshing and delightful—and perhaps in the same way that a small bit of honey is sufficient, a few words can go a long way. (Who, but a bear, gorges on honey?)

This is good news for fathers, most of whom don't have the same need for conversation that women do. The fact is, just listening, your very presence, and maybe a few well chosen words, a single sentence (as I learned from my dad) can be enough.

Here are six ways to speak gracious words into your daughter's life:

1. Tell her you see and hear her. When she initiates a conversation, don't just nod your head or glance in her direction, respond verbally and with your full attention. If you don't, she might think she's boring—or worse, that you don't care about her.

2. Tell her you admire her. I don't mean flatter her in an empty, insincere way. I mean notice internal qualities like thoughtfulness and creativity, kindness and honesty. When you see such traits in her, affirm them. Praise her. Say something like, "I noticed something about you today: You took your plate to the kitchen sink without having to be asked. Thanks for being so considerate." Or, "I saw how you were respectful to your mother when she got on you about your messy room. I like that. That's a great quality. I'm proud of you."

Don't focus on external things—her looks, athletic prowess, or academic accomplishment—but on her character. The world is always ready to acknowledge and reward (or disparage) what's outside, but it's up to a father to appreciate the girl behind the credentials or the looks. Someone has observed, "You cultivate that which you commend." That's true. Fathers who make a big deal out of superficial things are likely to have daughters who major in superficialities.

3. Tell her you love her. You probably can't say this too much. And while it's easier to say, "I love you" when she's little, she needs to hear it even more when she's older. Said sincerely, these three words can help stabilize an insecure heart, begin to heal a broken heart, and nourish a starving heart.

Don't say, "I love you because you're so beautiful and smart." If she wants a reason, tell her you love her because of who she is—a unique and precious soul.

4. Tell her stories from your life. You don't have to (and you shouldn't) share gory details, but tell her about times when you made mistakes and how you made those things right. Talk about lessons learned. Hearing about your experiences will give her courage—and the necessary wisdom—to face her own challenges.

5. Tell her your values. When you pass a billboard bearing bikini-clad models, talk about the virtue of modesty. When you hear a news story about a politician caught in a lie, talk about the importance of honesty. If she has a friend who becomes pregnant, remind her why you believe sex should be reserved for marriage. It's in unguarded, everyday moments like these that a father's words can have the greatest impact.

6. Tell her your hopes for her. This doesn't mean you try to program or plan out your daughter's life. It means you cast a vision for what her life can be. You paint a picture of a bright future.

Talk about how you hope she will always be a woman of integrity. Look her in the eyes and tell her that your prayer is that she will always be a faithful friend. When you hear a great story of someone who has succeeded because of determination and hard work, tell her, "You could do that."

My father knew my deep desire to become a physician, and he had confidence in me. My overhearing him tell that to a friend made all the difference.

My encouragement to you is this: Don't count on your daughter eavesdropping when you praise her to someone else. Tell her directly. Use the power of your words to speak grace into her life.

PRAY

God, help me find the right words, said at the right moment, and in the right spirit to bless and bring grace to my daughter. I love her and thank You for her life. Amen.

FLEX YOUR DAD MUSCLES

Commit yourself, today, to bring grace into your daughter's heart through conversation.

Don't worry if you don't communicate perfectly. If you're sincere, your daughter will know it, even if your words are clumsy.

Don't worry if she seems uninterested at first. She's listening more than you think.

Week 49

STAYING ALERT

For you are all children of the light and of the day;
we don't belong to darkness and night. So be on your guard,
not asleep like the others. Stay alert and be clearheaded.
—1 Thessalonians 5:5–6, NLT

When I was in college in the 1970s, a close friend of mine told me she didn't want to have children. "Bringing a child into such a crazy and uncertain world," she said, "would be irresponsible." All these years later, I continue to hear young married couples express this same sentiment.

My response is threefold: (1) This world has *always* been (and will always be) a frightening place for parents. (2) We should make big life decisions out of faith and strength, not fear. (3) If you take a look around, you'll see that many of those babies born during the tumultuous decades of the 1970s, '80s, and '90s not only survived childhood just fine but also became great parents themselves.

When it comes to fighting for child safety, I'll put my record up against anyone's. Believe me, as a mother, grandmother, and pediatrician, I well understand the angst parents feel when it comes to protecting their children. There is a world of bad stuff out there. Physically, morally, psychologically, and intellectually, our children face an array of serious threats to their well-being.

I know the drill. From the time our kids enter our homes until the time they leave, we worry constantly about them. Choking hazards, food allergies, accidents, diseases, sexual predators, peer pressure, drugs, alcohol, eating disorders, texting while driving (driving in general), the media, the Internet—the list of diverse and dizzying dangers seems endless. Fortunately we all have some daily distraction in the form of work and sleep. Otherwise we might be tempted to curl up in the fetal position, or pack up and move to some remote compound in the wilds of Alaska.

As toxic as our world is, though, *you* have the antidote. You can minimize the risks of your daughter finding trouble. And you don't have to stand by helplessly as it finds her. What's more, even if she is already in a tough spot, there are more resources available for you and her than ever before. So, keep your chin up. More important, keep your eyes open.

The Bible is filled with warnings for people to pay attention. For example, all people of faith are instructed: "Stay alert! Watch out for your great enemy, the devil. He prowls around like a roaring lion, looking for someone to devour" (1 Peter 5:8, NLT). It's imperative, Dad, for you to be vigilant, to realize the world is not entirely a benevolent place. Realize there are forces at work that, if left undetected and unchallenged, would gladly destroy your family.

In Isaiah 56:10, the leaders of the Jewish people are condemned. Why? Listen to the prophet's words: "For the leaders of my people—the LORD's watchmen, his shepherds—are blind and ignorant. They are like silent watchdogs that give no warning when danger comes. They love to lie around, sleeping and dreaming" (NLT).

Guess what? Though you may not be the leader of a nation, you are the protector of your family. You are a shepherd to your daughter. Never let such things be said about you.

In the New Testament, leaders are described this way: "Their work is to watch over your souls, and they are accountable to God" (Hebrews 13:17, NLT). While this passage was originally written to church leaders, this same job description applies to fathers as well.

What does staying alert look like for a father? What does it mean for you to watch over your daughter's soul? Among other things, it means you do the following:

Notice. When you talk to your daughter make sure the TV is off and the phone is put away. Multitasking is a farce. You can't pay attention to her with one eye and ear, and check e-mail or watch a game with the other. Face her. Make eye contact. Watch for facial clues. Listen to the words behind the words. Notice what she's not saying. Ask questions. Draw her out. You're probably keenly aware of every scratch or ding in your new car. Your daughter deserves the same attention.

Restrict. Don't allow your daughter to have a TV or computer in her room. Utilize Internet filters and channel block features on your TV. Don't let her log on to the Internet (even for homework) or watch TV unless one of her parents is present. Don't let her have a smartphone or e-mail or social media accounts when she's young. Before she loads any new app on her phone, make her clear it with you first. Set restrictions on the movies she can see. Never allow her to go to a party where alcohol is being served. In addition, older girls need age-appropriate guidelines regarding dating, driving, and so on. And all girls need parental supervision with regard to clothing. Daughters balk at all these restrictions, of course, but if you do it right, she will know deep down that you are doing such things to protect her, not punish her.

Monitor. Get to know your daughter's friends (and her friends' parents). If you allow her a smartphone, do it on the condition that you will monitor her texts. Similarly, if you allow your daughter to use Facebook, Twitter, Instagram, or other social media it must be on the condition that she allow you to "friend" and "follow" her. I warn you,

you and your wife will have to check this constantly. This is one place a girl can get in trouble quickly; you can't fall asleep on your watch. As the apostle Paul urged, "Be watchful, stand firm in the faith, act like men, be strong" (1 Corinthians 16:13, ESV). When your daughter is sixteen or seventeen, do not let her stay home alone on weekends, even if she's very responsible.

Warn. Whenever possible, in age-appropriate language, explain to your daughter the dangers in our world and the reasons for your rules and restrictions. You don't want her to be terrified, but you do want her to regard potential dangers with a healthy fear (the same kind of trepidation a young child has about touching a hot stove).

The key to helping our children thrive in a culture that continually lobs toxic messages at them is this: open your eyes so that you know what your daughter is up against. Then grab her hand and lead her through the challenge. Be alert and be available. That's it in a nutshell. It's so uncomplicated, yet so powerful. Your vigilant attention, your help, and your unswerving guidance are what your daughter needs to make it to adulthood relatively unscathed.

PRAY

God, I can't be too careful. It's an ugly world. Because of that, show me where I'm being too careless with my daughter. I am accountable to You to keep watch over her. Grant that I do that with the utmost care. Amen.

FLEX YOUR DAD MUSCLES

If you haven't already, find out how to block inappropriate channels or programs on your TV (you want blocks that not only deny access but block out the names of some highly offensive programming) and install an Internet filter on your family computer(s).

Then, go on a date with your wife (or if you're widowed or divorced, go out with a friend who has a daughter of similar age) and come up with a plan to become more vigilant and alert in protecting your daughters from the dangers of the world.

THE IMPACT OF STRONG FATHERS

LEAVING A LEGACY

*Jehoram was thirty-two years old when he
became king, and he reigned in Jerusalem eight years.
No one was sorry when he died.*
—2 Chronicles 21:20, NLT

That has to be one of the saddest verses in the Bible.

Jehoram was the eldest son of Jehoshaphat, one of Judah's preeminent kings. Jehoshaphat had left a legacy of being "deeply committed to the ways of the LORD" (2 Chronicles 17:6, NLT). He was famous for his desperate prayer during a time of national crisis: "We do not know what to do, but we are looking to you for help" (2 Chronicles 20:12, NLT).

Jehoram was nothing like his father. Upon assuming the throne in Jerusalem, he had all his younger brothers rounded up and executed. Then he proceeded to encourage the citizenry to engage in rampant idolatry. Here's how the Bible summarizes his eight-year reign: "He did evil in the eyes of the LORD" (2 Chronicles 21:6, NIV).

As prophesied by Elijah, Jehoram was eventually afflicted with a terrible intestinal disorder. Here's his epitaph:

> In the course of time, at the end of the second year, his bowels
> came out because of the disease, and he died in great pain. His

people made no funeral fire in his honor, as they had for his predecessors.... He passed away, to no one's regret. (2 Chronicles 21:19–20, NIV)

What a tragic legacy—to live in such a way that when you pass, nobody is really sorry to see you go. It's reminiscent of the old admonition: "When you were born, you cried and everyone else rejoiced; live in such a way that when you die, everyone else cries, and you rejoice."

I want you to think for a few moments about the important subject of leaving a legacy. A legacy is an inheritance. An inheritance is, most commonly, money or belongings or property you will to your heirs. But we leave behind immaterial valuables as well:

Memories to be treasured. Strong and smart dads realize that shared experiences are the greatest gift a father can give his child. No car or piece of jewelry will ever mean as much to your daughter as the memories of lunch dates and riding bikes and going to the zoo. One dad I know took his kids on a series of great road trips when they were young. They saw national parks, historic sites, and kitschy tourist traps too. His kids are grown now, but they still light up when talking about their adventures in the family minivan. Forget "stuff"; give your daughter the legacy of great memories. The hours and years you spend with her—or don't spend with her—change who she is.

Lessons you learned and shared. Another precious legacy you can give your daughter is to tell her your story. Open up about your highs and lows, your successes and failures. Share about your life, the things you've learned. Pass on the wisdom your own parents passed on to you—it's worth more than a big safety deposit box full of stock certificates and savings bonds. "For wisdom is more profitable than silver.... Wisdom is more precious than rubies" (Proverbs 3:14–15, NLT).

Skills you have passed on. A young mom in her mid-thirties was working with her husband, renovating the old house they had purchased in a foreclosure auction. When she reached in her tool apron to pull out her deceased dad's old tape measure, she teared up and smiled all at once as she was transported back to that summer in high school when she'd helped him convert part of the attic into a new bedroom for her. He taught her a lot of basic carpentry skills that she's used for almost two decades.

An example to emulate. Like it or not, every father is a role model, a template, a pattern. It's both nature (our kids have our DNA) and nurture (they live with us). Consequently, we can't help but mark them. Jesus put it this way: "But the student who is fully trained will become like the teacher" (Luke 6:40, NLT). If this is true in a teacher-student arrangement, how much more so in a parent-child relationship.

Every daughter receives the legacy (good or bad) of her father's example. You reproduce after your own kind. Your daughter may or may not resemble you in her physical appearance, but she will mimic your mannerisms, carry on your values, emulate your habits, copy (perhaps subconsciously) your traits, even ape your quirks.

So, leave her a good example. And remember, this has a ripple effect. Who else is watching you? Your son? Your daughter's friends? Perhaps other dads? Who knows, maybe your efforts will be the catalyst for a mini-movement of strong, active fathers. The Talmud says, "When you teach your son, you teach your son's son." We can amend that to say, "When you set a good example for your daughter, you set a good example for your granddaughter."

A faith to follow. More important than anything else, leave your daughter the legacy of a robust faith. Just as you teach her to ride a bike, or bait a hook, or stay away from drugs, or why it's important to treat others with dignity, teach her about God. Let her see your faith. Why? Because understanding God is the most important intellectual and spiritual discovery anyone can ever make.

In *Strong Fathers, Strong Daughters,* I wrote about the importance of your legacy: "One day, when she is grown, something between the two of you will shift. If you have done your job well, she will choose another good man to love her, fight for her, and be intimately connected to her. But he will never replace you in her heart, because you were there first. And that's the ultimate reward for being a good dad" (p. 237).

When your daughter leaves home, or when you leave your daughter to go to your ultimate home, make sure you leave her with a rich legacy.

PRAY

Almighty God, life is so fast. Make me aware. And, please, help me invest in my daughter every single day, so that when I'm gone, my daughter is rich in all the things that matter. Amen.

FLEX YOUR DAD MUSCLES

Get out your box of childhood memorabilia or pull out your old family photo albums (or pull them up digitally on your laptop—wherever you have them stored), and share some family history with your daughter. Pass on the stories your own parents passed on to you.

If you don't currently live in the place where you grew up (and if your hometown is not too far away), plan a weekend trip to show your daughter your roots. As you drive around your old stomping ground, tell her stories about events that transpired in various places. This will give her a deeper sense of her own heritage.

Perhaps you'd even like to begin doing some basic genealogical research with your daughter. (It's amazing what you can unearth online.)

NO GUARANTEES

Start children off on the way they should go,
and even when they are old they will not turn from it.
—Proverbs 22:6, NIV

In *Strong Fathers, Strong Daughters*, I relate the harrowing story of Ada. The youngest of three daughters, Ada was a good kid from a good home in the Midwest. She had a solid relationship with her parents, Alex and Mary, and never gave them any trouble—until high school.

At age fifteen, Ada began drifting away, despite the diligent efforts of her parents to stay connected to her. Alex took his daughter out for lunches, on movie dates, and even weekend getaways—but nothing halted her downward spiral.

At sixteen, Ada stole money from her parents and ran away. Alex hired a private detective, who located his daughter in San Diego. Alex flew west to retrieve Ada, but she refused to come with him. "If you force me home," she threatened, "I'll just run away again." She was working in a convenience store and living, she said, with a "friend" (whom Alex later learned was a divorced man almost twice her age). Heartbroken, Alex left California without his daughter.

A year to the day, Alex returned to see Ada, with whom he'd had zero contact. This time she was living in homeless shelters. She appeared to be sick. Again, she flatly refused his pleas to come home.

On Ada's eighteenth birthday, Alex made a third trip, only to discover his daughter living on the streets. Alex was convinced she was using drugs and possibly living as a prostitute. He desperately begged her to come home. Still she resisted.

This nightmarish pattern continued into Ada's early twenties. One day during a board meeting, Alex's cell phone rang. It was Ada! She was sobbing. When she told her dad she was at the train station in Grand Rapids, Michigan, Alex rushed from his meeting straight to her side. Bald and emaciated, Ada looked old and spent. But at last she was ready to come home.

Alex brought her home, where she began to try to put her life back together. At the same time, Ada and her parents began the grueling process of reconciliation. To this day, no one, not even Ada herself, understands why she did what she did.

In some ways, I suppose you could say this unhappy story has a positive ending. I tell it here to highlight the terrible uncertainty that is so much a part of being a parent.

As our children grow, we find we can no longer control them as we once could. (Remember restraining your flailing daughter against her will in her car seat or dressing her in sweet little outfits that you chose yourself?) With your daughter's increasing freedom comes the increasing possibility that she will make terrible choices (or at least choices you wouldn't make for her).

Sometimes we can intervene. Sometimes we can't (or shouldn't). You didn't want your daughter getting a tattoo, but there it is. Now what? You didn't want your daughter having sex before marriage, and, in fact, you repeatedly taught her not to engage in premarital sex; but now she's bawling her eyes out and telling you she's pregnant.

I talk with a lot of parents who like to quote the verse at the beginning of this chapter as an absolute child-rearing promise. *If I'm a good parent,* their reasoning goes, *that is, if I teach morals to my kid and take her to church, then there in Proverbs 22:6 is the heavenly guarantee she will turn out just fine. She will make good decisions. She will love God.*

Such "if...then" thinking sounds good to worried, struggling parents. We want it—desperately—to be true. But scholars are quick to point out that the biblical book of Proverbs isn't thirty-one chapters of *promises;* it's a collection of *truisms.* In other words, the proverbs aren't meant to be viewed as ironclad guarantees; rather, they are presented as generally true observations about how the world *normally* works. Always there are exceptions.

Remember original sin? It's proof that even God—the perfect and ultimate Father of us all—has messed-up kids. In the Bible, you'll find a host of godly parents who had godless kids. Mysteriously, the opposite is also true. You can find multiple instances in Scripture where evil parents somehow had children who were morally upstanding.

I'm not trying to be the bearer of bad news here. But I do feel the need to reiterate that there isn't some secret formula we can discover to be perfect parents of perfect children; there is no special "dad technique" you can employ that will *ensure* a certain outcome with your daughter.

What we do have are wise, biblical principles we can and should employ. I'm convinced that if you faithfully follow the wisdom God gives, all the while clinging to Him and trusting Him every step of the way, then you, my friend, are being a good parent. I don't know what the outcome—short-term or long-term—will be. But that's not our department anyway. Outcomes are, as the saying goes, above our pay grade. God simply wants us to do what He has called us to do, to do the best we can, and then trust Him to handle the rest.

As much as it makes me wince, and as much as I dislike saying it, I want to repeat: *there are no guaranteed outcomes.* If there were a secret formula for child-rearing, we wouldn't ever need to trust God.

Approach your role as a father with courage, faith, and humility. Persevere. Then remember, your daughter is ultimately responsible for her own choices. Do your part, and more times than not, all will turn out okay—but watching and waiting will often break your heart.

PRAY

God, grant me the fortitude to be the best father I can be, and to recognize that all ultimately rests in Your hands. Amen.

FLEX YOUR DAD MUSCLES

The well-known Serenity Prayer, often attributed to the theologian Reinhold Niebuhr, is an ideal prayer for fathers of daughters:

God, give me grace to accept with serenity
the things that cannot be changed,
Courage to change the things
which should be changed,
and the Wisdom to distinguish
the one from the other.

Living one day at a time,

Enjoying one moment at a time,

Accepting hardship as a pathway to peace,

Taking, as Jesus did,

This sinful world as it is,

Not as I would have it,

Trusting that You will make all things right,

If I surrender to Your will,

So that I may be reasonably happy in this life,

And supremely happy with You forever in the next.

Amen.

Week 52

THE FIGHT WORTH FIGHTING

*I have fought the good fight, I have finished the race,
and I have remained faithful.*
—2 Timothy 4:7, NLT

Religious scholars agree these are among the apostle Paul's final words. The aged apostle was imprisoned in Rome and probably beheaded shortly after penning this one last note to Timothy, his beloved protégé.

As far as anyone knows, Paul never married. He had no biological children. He never had the messy and miraculous experience of being a "daddy to a daughter." But he viewed Timothy as his "true son in the faith" (1 Timothy 1:2, NLT). When you read the letters Paul wrote in the New Testament, it's clear he had a father's heart.

As Paul contemplated the end of his life, he used rich and instructive language to describe his life experience—fighting "the good fight" and finishing "the race." What better metaphors than a "fight" and a "race" to describe a dad's job?

Fighting. Every day a man has to fight. (I can hear all the fathers murmuring their approval.) And it seems there is no cease-fire—ever. Work feels like all-out war sometimes. Then you head home, and lots of days it's not exactly quiet and peaceful on the family front. You tangle with your daughter over food and friends, bedtimes and boys, curfews and clothing. If you're like most fathers, you feel like you're fighting a losing battle with culture and technology (perhaps you still haven't figured out the difference between "tweeting" something and "pinning" something). To top it off, you are always trying to defend yourself against a million voices, internal and external, telling you what you should and should not be doing as a dad.

Here's what I want to say to you: Your daughter is worth the fight. In fact, every daughter wants to know if she is worth fighting for, and she wants her father to show her. Don't throw in the towel. Keep fighting the good fight. Keep advancing—moving toward your daughter with a desire to connect. Stay vigilant. Look for any hints of danger. Go on the attack against anything that might harm your daughter or hurt your relationship with her. She wants you in her life. She needs you to fight for her. When she leaves home you want to be able to smile and say with a clear conscience, "In my role as a father, I fought the good fight."

Racing. Notice Paul says, with a hint of victory in his voice, "I have finished the race." Earlier, in another letter (this one to the early Christians in Corinth, Greece), the apostle Paul borrowed imagery from the world of running to make a point about the need for discipline and perseverance in the life of faith:

> Don't you realize that in a race everyone runs, but only one person gets the prize? So run to win! All athletes are disciplined in their training. They do it to win a prize that will fade away, but we do it for an eternal prize. (1 Corinthians 9:24–25, NLT)

Raising a daughter is a race. But it's not a 100-meter dash (although, granted, in hindsight, childhood seems to last only about ten seconds).

In truth, raising your daughter is a long-distance run, a marathon. It takes discipline. It takes perseverance—an iron will to keep putting one foot in front of the other. And it takes stubborn determination—the steadfast refusal to quit. Fatherhood can be grueling, but the prize is great. If you've given fatherhood everything you've got, if you've taught your daughter about God, humility, integrity, and grit, she will be an amazing woman who has a deep impact on the world.

So don't stop running, Dad. Stay in the race, even when you feel like quitting—*especially* when you feel like quitting.

Ryan Hall, a veteran U.S. Olympic marathoner has said, "I don't think about the miles that are coming down the road, I don't think about the mile I'm on right now, I don't think about the miles I've already covered. I think about what I'm doing right now, just being lost in the moment."

That's great advice. Steve Prefontaine, the legendary long-distance runner who, at one time, held seven American track records, said, "To give anything less than your best is to sacrifice the gift." Your daughter is an amazing gift from God. She deserves your very best.

The finish line might be far off for you, but I promise the prize is worth it. As one unknown runner once said, "You will have dark days when you don't know if you can run a marathon…but if you don't quit, you will have a lifetime of joy knowing you did."

Remaining faithful. It was author Alvin Toffler who famously said, "Parenthood remains the greatest single preserve of the amateur." How true that is. As a parent you think, "What do I know? Why would the hospital knowingly send this child home with a clueless dad like me?" So, like a lot of parents, you scramble around looking for a secret formula or the magic shortcut for raising great kids. Books and conferences can offer wise principles, but those alone are worthless to a dad if he lacks one certain quality. Notice what Paul says.

After exclaiming, "I have fought the good fight, I have finished the race," Paul shares the secret to his success: "I have remained faithful." Here is the one indispensable ingredient for going the distance in life and in fatherhood: faithfulness.

Faithfulness means you keep showing up. You stay in the game—even when it's hard, when you don't feel like it, and when you'd rather be doing something else. Fighters and runners who do this, who consistently invest the time and effort, are the ones who ultimately enjoy success. They get to raise their hands in triumph. They would all tell you it's more than worth it.

Teddy Roosevelt once said, "There are many kinds of success in life worth having. It is exceedingly interesting and attractive to be a successful businessman, or railroad man, or farmer, or a successful lawyer or doctor; or a writer, or a president, or a ranchman, or the colonel of a fighting regiment, or to kill grizzly bears and lions. But for unflagging interest and enjoyment, a household of children... certainly makes all other forms of success and achievement lose their importance by comparison."

It comes down to what I wrote in *Strong Fathers, Strong Daughters*: "Every day is a challenge. The daily grind of work is tough.... Many days we are disappointed. We find ourselves grasping for that elusive 'something' that will make us feel more complete. But the more we search for it, the more distant it becomes, because what we're searching for is sitting right there. It's not your job or your hobbies. It's not more money or more sex. It's your family—your children, your spouse—and God. They are the real center of our lives. Men who figure this out find what they're looking for. Men who don't are never truly happy and satisfied" (p. 231). A strong father is a happy father.

PRAY

God, help me to emulate the apostle Paul in fighting the good fight and running the race, remaining always faithful to You and to my duties as a father. Amen.

FLEX YOUR DAD MUSCLES

The only thing to do at this point is *go do*. Get started. Skim back over these pages. Note the things you've highlighted. Reread the notes you've scribbled in the margin. Pick one actionable item, and do it today. In fact, do it right now. Be a strong dad. Raise your daughter to be a strong woman. And give the glory to God.

ACKNOWLEDGMENTS

I would like to extend my deepest thanks and gratitude to my agent and friend Shannon Litton. Thank you for your constant encouragement, wisdom, and support. To my dear friend and assistant Anne Mann, thank you for your steadfast spirit and dedication to Jesus and me. I thank Marji Ross for her suggestion to write about fathers and daughters and Harry Crocker—the best editor in the business—for his help with the original manuscript. I am grateful to Bob DeMoss at Regnery for pursuing the dream of writing a devotional on this topic as well as Chris Hudson and Len Woods for their writing expertise.

Finally, I'd like to thank my friend Dave Ramsey for his enthusiasm for the original text and James Dobson for championing families over the past four decades. Both of you inspire me to keep writing and speaking out on behalf of good men.

SOURCES

WEEK 12: COMPASSION

Adapted from "The Power of Dad," at Dr. James Dobson's Family Talk website and, "Q&A: Dr. Meg Meeker on 'Strong Fathers, Strong Daughters,'" Human Events, October 10, 2006, http://humanevents.com/2006/10/10/qa-dr-meg-meeker-on-strong-fathers-strong-daughters/.

WEEK 18: GENEROSITY

Adapted from "Want to Shake Up Your Life?," at Dr. James Dobson's Family Talk website.

Week 33: Discipline

Adapted from The 12 Principles of Raising Great Kids from The Strong Parent Project online program, Principle 2: "Discipline with Courage and Kindness."

Week 34: Getting off the Crazy Train

Adapted from The 12 Principles of Raising Great Kids from The Strong Parent Project online program, Principle 1: "Three Questions Your Child Needs Answered."

Week 37: Liking

Adapted from Your Kids at Risk: How Teen Sex Threatens Our Sons and Daughters, pp. 197–99.

Week 39: Picking Your Battles

Adapted from The 12 Principles of Raising Great Kids from The Strong Parent Project online program.

Week 40: Practicing Gratitude

Adapted in part from a blog on the website.

Week 43: Protecting

Adapted from "Navigating Our Big Scary World" from The 12 Principles of Raising Great Kids from The Strong Parent Project online program.

WEEK 44: SERVING

Adapted from *Strong Fathers, Strong Daughters: The 30-Day Challenge*, days 11 and 12.

WEEK 45: SETTING BOUNDARIES

Adapted from The 12 Principles of Raising Great Kids from The Strong Parent Project online program.

WEEK 46: SHOWING AFFECTION

Adapted from Your Kids at Risk: How Teen Sex Threatens Our Sons *and Daughters*, pp. 201–2.

WEEK 49: STAYING ALERT

Adapted from The 12 Principles of Raising Great Kids from The Strong Parent Project online program.

NOTES

NOTES

NOTES

NOTES

NOTES

NOTES

NOTES

NOTES

NOTES